Modern Political Economic Conditions

by

Nicholas Jay Boyes

Nicholas Jay Boyes

www.ecologicalera.com

ISBN: 978-0-359-31159-0

Sections

History

Christian religion is what Islam was based on; it forms an important part of the monotheistic faith, as Christians share with Muslims their dislike for the ancients. Both considered the polytheistic religions, for example what existed in Mecca when Mohammad, the Islamic messenger of God was alive, as dangerous to their following. Mohammad felt he had to conquer Mecca with his following after Satan had gained control of him there. The Satanic Verses in Islam refer to when Mohammad went to Mecca, and promised that the polytheistic religion would be safe under Islam. There were the up and down prayers, and the agreement was made. This was until Mohammad went home to Medina a few days later, and it became clear this was not acceptable to the Islamic movement. The Muslims then said Mohammad was under the influence of Satan in Mecca, with the implied conclusion that polytheistic faiths are the devil. Christians also felt the ancients were heathen, and destroyed many ancient sites throughout the Middle East prior to Satan possessing Mohammad.

The Islamic State organization took Palmyra in April of 2018, one of the few intact ruins of the ancient world.

The title Heathen was applied by the followers of Christ to the ancient societies such as the Greeks and Romans. The opposition to the ancient culture is one of the strongest messages sent by the Christians, and their progeny Islam. Palmyra was sacked, and the ruins bore further damage from Islamic State. The ruins were deemed dangerous, and the columns and arches no longer stand in Palmyra, Syria.

It has a parallel in history to early Christians, who sacked ancient sites, including two of the seven wonders of civilization, the library of Alexandria, and the Temple of Apollo.

"By the 4th century, Delphi had acquired the status of a city, which was located to the west of the sanctuary grounds. Constantine the Great looted several monuments, most notably the Tripod of Plataea, which he used to decorate his new capital, Constantinople.

http://en.wikipedia.org/wiki/Delphi#History

Constantine was the first emperor of Rome to convert to Christianity when this destruction occurred in the fourth century AD. Constantinople, what was Byzantium and Chalcidis, would be named after this leader of the Christians. Prior to this there was a fire at Delphi, but this direct looting of the temple was the start of the eventual destruction of the Temple of Delphi, one of the most important religious sites of the ancient world, by the new faith Christianity. The Tripod of Plataea was a monument built by the Greeks containing three intertwined snakes that symbolized the 31 Greek city states that fought the Persians in the Greco Persian wars that lasted between 499 BC and 449 BC. Made from the melted down Bronze weapons used by the Persians, according to Herodotus the monument was placed near the Oracle as a tribute to the God Apollo.

"The temple (of Apollo) survived until AD 390, when the Roman emperor Theodosius I silenced the oracle by destroying the temple and most of the statues and works of art in the name of Christianity. The site was completely destroyed by zealous Christians in an attempt to remove all traces of Paganism.

http://en.wikipedia.org/wiki/Delphi#Temple_of_Apollo

The ascension of Christians to the Roman empire resulted in the destruction of this magnificent temple. It was viewed as a heathen monument and destroyed by early Christians. Thus the end of the temple of Delphi.

Christians, as detailed in the documentary film Agora by the Spanish Ministry of Culture, also destroyed the Great Library of Alexanderia. The librarian Hypatia was killed, and the contents of the library, the most important and largest in the ancient world was burned down. The hatred of ancients by the Christians formed what led to the Dark Ages, when Roman industry that linked the city states of Western Europe together for centuries collapsed. The Romans prior to this had settled many regions in Western Europe, and their industry built many of the roads that linked Rome to the rest of the world. The complete loss of order culminates in the fall of Rome, and for about a thousand years Europe would be decentralized states under of rival Princes, often referred to as the Dark Ages.

The fall of Rome:

"Flavius Odoacer, also known as Flavius Odovacer (Italian: Odoacre, Latin: Odoacerus German: Odoaker), was a soldier, who in 476 became the first King of Italy (476–493). His reign is commonly seen as marking the end of the Western Roman Empire.... He was an Arian Christian.... Most sources today claim that he was most likely of Germanic stock.... The presence of successor states controlled by a nobility from one of the Germanic tribes is evident in the 6th century...

History

Wikipedia Germanic people

Odoacer had the support of Constantinople to depose the emperor Romulus Augustulus, which he did when he took power in AD 476. By this time most of the important sites of the ancients had followed the pattern of the Temple of Apollo and the Great Library of Alexandria, destruction by Christians of the monuments they called Pagan. This led to the Dark Ages, which refers to the lack of records after the fall of the Roman Empire, which lasted until the Renaissance. It is thought that Odoacer could not read or write. It was in this period in the East Islam would form.

The religion of Islam was founded by Mohammad (570 – 632 AD) as an offshoot of Christianity, as a monotheistic faith. It is still alive today, and of late its following has continued to attempt to rewrite history by destroying ancient monuments they call pagan.

The destruction of Palmyra by Islamic State was a further offense against the ancients, who are still called Pagan by Islam. The new religion seems to have settled nothing as regards Christian beliefs that led to the fall of Rome, reconciliation was never achieved with the groups called Pagan. If anything Islam is more extreme than Christianity, as their messenger of God Mohammad was a military leader against the Quraysh, whose city was originally called Yathrid. It would be renamed Mecca when in 629 Quraysh rule ended and Mohammad's army conquered the city. Jihad, holy war, seems to be written into the new religion, which was what Mohammad's battle represents to Islam. In the Quran there are many scriptures that refer to among other things of thousands of angels joining Mohammad's army to conquer the Quryah. Apparently according to the Hadith, a record of Mohammad's words, he refers to the angel Jibreel supporting him in his conquest.

Christians often deny slavery went away when Rome was Christianized. In Agora the slaves overthrow the Romans, resulting in the destruction of the Great Library of Alexandria. That the slaves became Christians, and overthrew their masters. Clearly they were taken as fools, as slavery was not abolished by the Christians, it continued well into the 19th century.

"Venice was far from the only slave trading hub in Italy. Southern Italy boasted slaves from distant regions, including Greece, Bulgaria, Armenia, and Slavic regions. During the 9th and 10th centuries, Amalfi (Italy) was a major exporter of slaves to North Africa. Genoa, along with Venice, dominated the trade in the Eastern

Mediterranean beginning in the 12th century, and in the Black Sea beginning in the 13th century. They sold both Slavic and Baltic slaves, as well as Georgians, Turks, and other ethnic groups of the Black Sea and Caucasus, to the Muslim nations of the Middle East. Genoa primarily managed the slave trade from Crimea to Mamluk Egypt, until the 13th century, when increasing Venetian control over the Eastern Mediterranean allowed Venice to dominate that market. Between 1414 and 1423 alone, at least 10,000 slaves were sold in Venice.

".., slavery thrived as an institution in medieval Christian Iberia. Slavery existed in the region under the Romans, and continued to do so under the Visigoths. From the fifth to the early 8th century, large portions of the Iberian Peninsula were ruled by Christian Visigothic Kingdoms whose rulers worked to codify human bondage. In the 7th century, King Chindasuinth issued the Visigothic Code (Liber Iudiciorum), to which subsequent Visigothic kings added new legislation. Although the Visigothic Kingdom collapsed in the early 8th century, portions of the Visigothic Code were still observed in parts of Spain in the following centuries. The Code, with its pronounced and frequent attention to the legal status of slaves, reveals the continuation of slavery as an institution in post-Roman Spain.

"The Code regulated the social conditions, behavior, and punishments of slaves in early medieval Spain. The marriage of slaves and free or freed people was prohibited. Book III, title II, iii ("Where a Freeborn Woman Marries the Slave of Another or a Freeborn Man the Female Slave of Another") stipulates that if a free woman marries another person's slave, the couple is to be separated and given 100 lashes. Furthermore, if the woman refuses to leave the slave, then she becomes the property of the slave's master. Likewise, any children born to the couple would follow the father's condition and be slaves.

Wikipedia Slavery in Medieval Europe

Which clearly shows the Christian movement that caused slave revolt in Egypt, which led to the destruction of the Great Library of Alexandria, did not end slavery. It is questionable if they were ever serious about doing it. Throughout the history of Europe, and well into the Inquisition, slaves were traded from Europe to the Ottoman Empire, to the Americas later. In the Middle Ages slavery was alive and well, although serfdom and indentured labour was far more common. The master apprentice journeyman relationships of the Guild and the corporation would reign in the Middle Ages in the cities. But on the land serfdom was the most common from of property, with most people working the soil. Inherited titles to land ownership was the rule, born into.

Asiatic Society in Modern Times

It is historical to note the old Asiatic societies still exist in the new millennium. In Western Asia, referred to as the Middle East, the old Asiatic society is still alive.

These societies are monarchies, and the women are expected to wear clothing that designates them as female supporters of the religion there, Islam. It is the veil, and it is worn by Muslim women in the kingdom as a symbol of their faith in the religion and the kingdom.

The leaders of the society have many wives, and they bear children. In Saudi Arabia, the harem was still practiced by the Muslim nobles in the 20th century. The children produced by the harem all had the same father.

"The Ottomans employed eunuchs as guardians of the harem. Istanbul's Topkapı Palace housed several hundred eunuchs in the late-sixteenth century. The head eunuch who guarded the entrance of the harem was known as kızlar ağası. Eunuchs were either Nilotic slaves captured in the Nile vicinity and transported through ports in Upper Egypt, the Sudan and Abyssinia, or European slaves such as Slavs and Franks.

"The Imperial Harem of the Ottoman sultan, which was also called seraglio in the West, was part of Topkapı Palace. It also housed the Valide Sultan, as well as the sultan's daughters and other female relatives. Eunuchs and servant girls were also part of the harem. During the later periods, the sons of the sultan lived in the Harem until they were 12 years old.

Wikipedia Harem

This practice of nobility having harems is part of feudalism, and surviving today. Here we have an example of living feudalism in the modern era:

"Al Fayez, a descendant of a well-to-do Jordanian family, recalls the first time she saw Abdullah. (King Abdullah bin Abdulaziz ed.) It was 1972. She was 15, he was 48, and she was told that he would be her husband.

"I was being given to him in marriage," she says. "It was arranged."

"Despite the riches and the servants and the pampering, life quickly became "monotonous," she says. Almost immediately, she got pregnant.

""After I was forced to marry him, Abdullah would come to my room as a visitor for a few hours every now and then," Al Fayez says. "And then he'd go to his other wives, so you don't even fight, you don't even matter."

"Abdullah, who has had 30 wives and fathered more than 40 children, finally divorced Al Fayez sometime in the 1980s — but she didn't find out until two years later, through an intermediary. In Saudi Arabia, a husband can divorce his wife without her knowledge.

"When it comes to the rights of women, Saudi Arabia has one of the worst human-rights records in the world. Women don't have a say in raising their children. They can't go to school, travel, open a bank account, conduct any kind of business or get medical treatment — especially gynecological surgery — without male permission.

New York Post April 19, 2014

Saudi Arabia has decided to retain complete control of their petroleum, with Aramco no longer becoming partially a joint stock company. Of late they have suspended offering 5% of the company to investors. It is owned by the King, and is property of the royal family. A massive industry ruled by a feudal power, with titles to hereditary ownership, just like the Middle ages in Europe.

*"The **House of Saud** (Arabic:, Āl Su'ūd IPA: [ʔaːl soʕuːd]) is the ruling royal family of Saudi Arabia. It is composed of the descendants of Muhammad bin Saud, founder of the Emirate of Diriyah, known as the First Saudi state (1744–1818), and his brothers, though the ruling faction of the family is primarily led by the descendants of Ibn Saud, the modern founder of Saudi Arabia. The most influential member of the Royal family is the King of Saudi Arabia, currently King Salman, who chose first his nephew and then his son as crown prince.... The family is estimated to comprise 15,000 members, but the majority of the power and wealth is possessed by a group of about 2,000 of them.*

"House of Saud is a translation of Al Saud, an Arabic dynastic name formed by adding the word Al, meaning "family of" or "House of", to the personal name of an ancestor. In the case of the Al Saud, this is Saud ibn Muhammad ibn Muqrin, the father of the dynasty's 18th century founder, Muhammad bin Saud (Muhammad, son of Saud).

"Today, the surname "Al Saud" is carried by any descendant of Muhammad bin Saud or his three brothers Farhan, Thunayyan, and Mishari.

Wikipedia House of Saud

The descendants of Muhammad bin Saud are in powerful positions. The harem is still practiced, although it is now a secret, it is not like in the past where it was a open accepted practice. In the past kings often had dozens of wives, and had all of them bearing his children. Thus the House of Saud being the royal family is a large unit, comprising the leadership of the state, all descendants of the monarch's wives in the royal harem, about a hundred children. Ibn Saud fathered many children, including 45 sons, and all of the subsequent kings of Saudi Arabia.

11 of King Abdulaziz Ibn Saud would inherit hereditary titles to land ownership, which would ultimately be used for mining of petroleum. Seven would become kings, including King Salman who currently is the leader of Saudi Arabia. His son Mohamed Bin Salman is Crown Prince, and is powerful enough to be considered leader of the country by many.

The nobles control the industry, dominated by petroleum, which is still plentiful in the Middle East. The largest oil manufacturing industry in the world is in Saudi Arabia, Arab American Oil Company, now known as Aramco manufacturing. The royal family owns it although is part of the state. It is the Crown Jewels.

The state and the religion are not separate, Islam is the state religion. The practice of Islam has an activity attached to it by Saudi Arabia, the Pilgrimage to Mecca. It is considered the duty of all Muslim men to go to the Hajj, a visit to Mecca for an annual religious ritual. Women pilgrims have to be accompanied by a "Mahram," a male Muslim partner. Without a Mahram, the pilgrimage of a woman is not considered valid. In fact the Saudi government does not allow women below the age of 45 to undertake the pilgrimage if they do not have a male guardian.

The Saudis have constructed monuments for the Hajj, the pillars for stoning Satan, for instance. Muslim men are expected to stone Satan at the gathering. It is considered to be a duty of all Muslim men to attend the Haj and stone the devil. The Saudis have constructed elaborate structures to accommodate the millions of Muslims who arrive every year in honor of the warrior Mohammed who conquered Mecca. He is still viewed as a living representative of god, like Jesus Christ.

Asiatic Society and Modern Material Conditions

So the old Asiatic society is still alive in the Middle East. Its monotheistic religion, Islam, descended from Christianity, continues to be practiced in the entire region.

Having hereditary titles land ownership and class in the old world, Princes, Kings, Crown Princes, etc. all part of feudalism that has been virtually unchanged since Medieval times.

These titles to land ownership and personal relationships are not capitalism. The position of wage labour in these patriarchal societies is open to question.

According to the U.S. State Department as of 2005:

"Saudi Arabia is a destination for men and women from South and East Asia and East Africa trafficked for the purpose of labor exploitation, and for children from Yemen, Afghanistan, and Africa... Hundreds of thousands of low-skilled workers from India, Indonesia, the Philippines, Sri Lanka, Bangladesh, Ethiopia, Eritrea, and Kenya migrate voluntarily to Saudi Arabia; some fall into conditions of involuntary servitude, suffering from physical and sexual abuse, non-payment or delayed payment of wages, the withholding of travel documents, restrictions on their freedom of movement" and non-consensual contract alterations. The Government of Saudi Arabia does not comply with the minimum standards for the elimination of trafficking and is not making significant efforts to do so.

according to Wikipedia:

"A system of plantation labor, much like that which would emerge in the Americas, developed early on, but with such dire consequences that subsequent engagements were relatively rare and reduced. Moreover, the need for agricultural labor, in an Islamic world with large peasant populations, was nowhere near as acute as in the Americas. Slaves in Islam were mainly directed at the service sector — concubines and cooks, porters and soldiers — with slavery itself primarily a form of consumption rather than a factor of production. The most telling evidence for this is found in the gender ratio; among black slaves traded in Islamic empire across the centuries, there were roughly two females to every male. Almost all of these female slaves had domestic occupations. For some, this also included sexual relations with their masters. This was a lawful motive for their purchase, and the most common one.

Modern Political Economic Conditions by Nicholas Jay Boyes

"Slavery was a legal and important part of the economy of the Ottoman Empire and Ottoman society until the slavery of Caucasians was banned in the early 19th century, although slaves from other groups were allowed. In Constantinople (present-day Istanbul), the administrative and political center of the Empire, about a fifth of the population consisted of slaves in 1609. Even after several measures to ban slavery in the late 19th century, the practice continued largely unfazed into the early 20th century. As late as 1908, female slaves were still sold in the Ottoman Empire. Sexual slavery was a central part of the Ottoman slave system throughout the history of the institution.

"In 1962 practicing slavery... in Saudi Arabia was prohibited.

Wikipedia History of Slavery in the Muslim World

Ibid.

Which really makes one wonder what the motivation is for becoming Muslim to black Americans. Islam also had black slaves until the 20th century, the owner of a slave considered him his property, and the essence of the relationship was the slave was not paid. Slaves in Muslim countries were different from slaves in Western society, they were more for servants and sex than as plantation workers. Thus they were treated different than the black slaves of the Americas, the latter were brought to the Americas because they were big and strong, and the labour on Cotton and Sugar plantations was very demanding. Most European men could not handle working in the sun in tropical climates doing strenuous work like working the crops. Slaves in the Muslim world were often used for sex by their masters, something far less common in the Americas. The title of slave described the role in society of the human being who was not paid for his labour, feudal titles allowed for owning slaves.

The very essence of medieval culture was personal titles governing relationships, master servant, etc. The presence of princes implies titles inherited for many years, in many cases when feudalism was the more dominant force in society, as opposed to wage labour and capitalism, which dominates European and American society today.

In this respect we see the cultural values of feudalism, chastity, male dominance, religion etc. all still present in the old Asiatic society. The religion cannot be separated from this; it is a product of feudal society, descended from monotheistic Christianity. There is even a clothing to show a woman is a Muslim practitioner; a

16

Burka or headscarf to symbolize their support for patriarchal Islamic society and the cultural values just mentioned. They are not much different from the early Christians, both have a human messenger of God, first Jesus Christ then Mohammad.

The old Asiatic society has recently been a source of petroleum, which has brought industrial development to many of the more remote regions, often in the desert. But feudal titles remain; Crown Prince and King govern in Saudi Arabia, Kuwait, Jordan, Qatar, Oman, Bahrain, and United Arab Emirates. Thus we see that feudalism is alive and well into the new millennium...

Large corporations doing manufacture are present in Saudi Arabia:

"Saudi Aramco, *officially the Saudi Arabian Oil Company most popularly known just as Aramco (formerly Arabian-American Oil Company), is a Saudi Arabian petroleum and natural gas company based in Dharan. Saudi Aramco's market value has been estimated at between $2 trillion and $10 trillion, making it the most valuable company in the world.*

Saudi Aramco Wikipedia

While slavery may not be present in this company, it is not clear what a feudal kingdom owning the largest industry means for wage labour. Saudi Arabia is feudalism, the fact it is connected to the state tells us nothing, it is owned by King Salman.

In bourgeois society there are still many things persisting from history that resemble the old Asiatic society, with its titles and patriarchal culture. Perhaps that is why Western powers spend so much time and material efforts there. The patriarchal society seems to be given bourgeois support in military matters. Perhaps the two are not so far apart.

Petroleum and Material Conditions

The use of fossil fuels, petroleum in particular, has led to the rise and fall of empires. In the countries with petroleum in the ground, Iran, for instance, petroleum was connected to revolutions, and the fall of a 2500-year-old monarchy in the Islamic revolution.

"Mosaddegh (16 June 1882 – 5 March 1967) was an Iranian politician and the leader of the movement to nationalize Iran's oil industry. He was educated in Europe, and joined politics after the Iranian Constitutional Revolution of 1905-1907. He held multiple posts such as member of parliament, governor of the Fars province, finance minister, foreign minister, and prime minister. In the election of the 14th Majlis in 1943, he was elected member for Tehran. Before gaining recognition as the leader of the national oil movement, he played a large role in the trans-Iranian railway project and the re-organization of the courts and the Justice Department.

"The 16th Majlis consisted of some members from National Front such as Mosaddegh. In November 1950, the rejection of the oil supplemental agreement was offered from the oil committee of Majlis which was chaired by Mosaddegh. The prime minister at the time, Haj Ali Razmara, opposed the measure. On March 7, 1951, Razmara was murdered by Khalil Tahmasebi, a member of Fada'iyan-e Islam. After the death of Razmara, the Majlis began the process of nationalizing the Iranian oil industry.

"On March 15, 1951, legislation to nationalize the oil industry was passed by the Majlis with a majority of votes. On March 17 the Majlis verified the nationalization of Iran oil industry and the AIOC (Anglo Iranian Oil Company) was nationalized.

Wikipedia Nationalization of the Iranian Oil Industry

The struggle to nationalize the oil has been occurring for decades, with continual efforts by western capitalists to control the fields. These early attempts for Iran to own the petroleum under their feet mark one of the earliest tries to remove the ownership of the petroleum from large capitalists to the Iranian workers.

...in March 1951, the Iranian parliament (the Majlis) voted to nationalise the Anglo-Iranian Oil Company (AIOC) and its holdings, and shortly thereafter the Iranian

public elected a champion of nationalisation, Mohammed Mossadegh, Prime Minister. This led to the Abadan Crisis, in which, under British pressure, foreign countries agreed not to purchase Iranian oil, and the Abadan refinery was closed. The AIOC withdrew from Iran and increased the output of its other reserves in the Persian Gulf.

"Mossadegh's opposition caused the British to conclude that he had to go. Officials at the Ministry of Fuel and Power wrote in September 1951:

"If Dr. Mussadiq (sic) resigns or is replaced, it is just possible that we shall be able to get away from outright nationalization ... It would certainly be dangerous to offer greater real control of oil operations in Persia. Although something might be done to put more of a Persian facade on the setup, we must not forget that the Persians are not so far wrong when they say that all our proposals are, in fact, merely dressing up the AIOC control in other clothing ... Any real concession on this point is impossible. If we reached settlement on Mussadiq's terms, we would jeopardise not only British but also American oil interests throughout the world. We would destroy prospects of the investments of foreign capital in backward countries. We would strike a fatal blow to international law. We have a duty to stay and use force to protect our interest ... We must force the Shah to bring down Mussadiq.

Wikipedia Anglo Persian Oil Company

Just what exactly is meant by "investments in backward countries" is open to question. Sounds pretty bourgeois, more of a capitulation to capitalists so recently rejected in the Second World War. Were they in cooperation with the bourgeoisie, allowing for capitalists to invest in less developed countries to make large profits? It certainly is embarrassing by today's standards. Of course, nationalized oil is still being fought about currently, Iraq, for example.

"Britain was unable to subvert Mossadegh as its embassy and officials had been evicted from Iran in October 1952, but successfully appealed in the US to exaggerated anti-communist sentiments, depicting both Mossadegh and Iran as unstable and likely to fall to communism as they were weakened. If Iran fell, the "enormous assets" of "Iranian oil production and reserves" would fall into communist control, as would "in short order the other areas of the Middle East". By 1953 both the US and the UK had new, more anti-communist and interventionist administrations and the United States no longer opposed intervention in Iran.

Wikipedia ibid.

It's strange to see the same person who befriended the Soviet Union, Churchill become against nationalized oil. And justifying it by some of the same logic that led Adolf Hitler to march to the east. The only question left is what exactly he thought about Jews, considering he was against the Communist Party, who accepted the Jews in the war. By 1953 American had long since unfriended the socialists. By 1953 the Korean War would be ending with a stalemate, Japan's old colony divided between nationalized property in the east and capitalist land tenure arrangements in the west. Korea would slowly disintegrate with father passing power to son, and son passing power to son, ending attempts at becoming some form of socialism. It should be noted Britain and America were not worker revolutions in or prior to the war, although they were bourgeois supporters of working class movements in Europe.

"The anti-Mossadegh plan was orchestrated under the code-name 'Operation Ajax' by CIA, and 'Operation Boot' by SIS (MI6). In August, the American CIA with the help of bribes to politicians, soldiers, mobs, and newspapers, and information from the British embassy and secret service, organized a riot which gave the Shah an excuse to remove Mosaddeq.

"The Shah seized the opportunity and issued an edict forcefully removing the immensely popular and democratically elected Mosaddeq from power when General Fazlollah Zahedi led tanks to Mosaddeq's residence and arrested him. On 21 December 1953, he was sentenced to death but his sentence was later commuted to three years' solitary confinement in a military prison followed by life in prison. He was kept under house arrest at his Ahmadabad residence, until his death, on 5 March 1967

"With a pro-Western Shah and the new pro-Western Prime Minister, Fazlollah Zahedi, Iranian oil began flowing again and the Anglo-Iranian Oil Company, which changed its name to British Petroleum in 1954, tried to return to its old position. However, public opinion was so opposed that the new government could not permit it.

"Under pressure from the United States, British Petroleum was forced to accept membership in a consortium of companies which would bring Iranian oil back on the international market. It was incorporated in London in 1954 as a holding company called Iranian Oil Participants Ltd (IOP). The founding members of IOP included British Petroleum (40%), Gulf Oil (8%), Royal Dutch Shell (14%), and Compagnie Française des Pétroles (later Total S.A., 6%). The four Aramco partners—Standard Oil of California (SoCal, later Chevron), Standard Oil of New Jersey (later Exxon),

Standard Oil Co. of New York (later Mobil, then ExxonMobil), and Texaco—each held an 8% stake in the holding company.

Wikipedia ibid.

Much like Iraq of late the nationalized petroleum would be expropriated, and the profits from pumping it out of the ground in the hands of capitalists. In this case the feudal power, the Shah, was involved in removal of a popular leader. Britain and America supported this, and we are left trying to figure out if Britain thought Iran was so backward why they would support the Shah, who clearly represented the most backward tendencies of Persia.

"Following the (1979 Islamic) Revolution, the NIOC (the National Iranian Oil Company) took control of Iran's petroleum industry and canceled Iran's international oil agreements. In 1980 the exploration, production, sale, and export of oil were delegated to the Ministry of Petroleum. Initially Iran's post-revolutionary oil policy was based on foreign currency requirements and the long-term preservation of the natural resource. Following the Iran–Iraq War, however, this policy was replaced by a more aggressive approach: maximizing exports and accelerating economic growth. From 1979 until 1998, Iran did not sign any oil agreements with foreign oil companies. Early in the first administration of President Mohammad Khatami (in office 1997–2005), the government paid special attention to developing the country's oil and gas industry. Oil was defined as inter-generational capital and an indispensable foundation of economic development.

Wikipedia Economic History of Iran

The Islamic Revolutionaries nationalized Iran's oil industry eventually. The first Persian attempt at nationalizing petroleum in 1951 might have worked, but Iran was not a strong country then, although in World War Two it was a useful oil production region for the Soviet Union. To nationalize the oil more than a move in Parliament was needed, a real revolution had to occur before the oil would become property of Iran's workers.

Thus the opposition to Iran by the Saudi's. Saudi Arabian oil is the property of the King, the royalty use it to maintain power and wealth. They are still at loggerheads about it, and fighting in Yemen with American made weapons.

History - Petroleum and Material Conditions

Other than China who produces oil in Iran today, most all of Iran's oil is nationalized production. The bourgeois still to this day have a war of words going with Iran's leadership, the roots of which obviously go back to the last century...

Iraq would discover oil in 1927, by the Ottoman Empire's Turkish Petroleum Company (TPC). In the years that followed the country would have its oil fields owned by many western companies.

"The discovery hastened the negotiations over the composition of TPC, and on 31 July 1928 the shareholders signed a formal partnership agreement to include the Near East Development Corporation (NEDC), an American consortium of five large US oil companies that included Standard Oil of New Jersey, Standard Oil Company of New York (Socony), Gulf Oil, the Pan-American Petroleum and Transport Company, and Atlantic Richfield Co. Shares were held in the following proportions: 23.75% each to the Anglo-Persian Oil Company, Royal Dutch/Shell, the Compagnie Française des Pétroles(CFP), and the NEDC; the remaining 5% went to Calouste Gulbenkian (the Turkish ed.).

Wikipedia Iraq Oil Company

The Turkish Petroleum Company TPC was 23.75% owned by American capitalists Standard Oil of New Jersey, Standard Oil Company of New York (Socony), Gulf Oil, the Pan-American Petroleum and Transport Company, and Atlantic Richfield Co. by 1928. In 1929 the TPC was renamed the Iraq Petroleum Company (IPC). The IPC capitalists would gain license to explore oil throughout the Middle East, and find it. By 1948 it was a large industry.

"During the Hashemite Monarchy (1932–58), there were no serious issues between the IPC and the Iraqi government as the Hashemites were extremely pro-west. In fact, they had been installed by the British, and therefore tensions were minimized. They were dependent on the British militarily and had essentially pledged allegiance to them through the Baghdad Pact.

"This atmosphere did not continue to the negotiations held between the IPC and revolutionary governments that followed the overthrow of the Hashemite monarchy in 1958."

Wikipedia ibid.

Qasim was the military leader who replaced the Hashemite monarchy, who wanted to nationalize Iraq's petroleum.

"On 12 December 1961, the Iraqi government enacted Law No. 80, which expropriated 99.5 per cent of the IPC group's concession areas without compensation and put an immediate stop on oil exploration. One major difference between these negotiations and those of 1952, was the stance of the Iraqi government. Whereas it had been more willing to accommodate the IPC in 1952, the government's positions under Qasim were largely non-negotiable. However this should not be surprising because it was expected that Qasim would take advantage of growing Arab nationalism and a sense amongst many ordinary Iraqis that they were being exploited by the west.

"Throughout the 1960s, the Iraqi government criticized the IPC and used the IPC as a central piece of their anti-western propaganda. The Soviet-Iraqi agreement of 1969 emboldened the Iraqi government and in 1970 they made a list of demands including ownership of 20% of the company's assets and more control. The IPC by this time was taking the Iraqi government very seriously and made some huge concessions. They agreed to increase oil production substantially and also increase the price of its crude oil in certain areas. They also offered an advance payment on royalties.

"However this was not enough for the Iraqi government and they issued a new set of demands in November 1970 which essentially involved more Iraqi control of operations and more Iraqi profit-taking. Dissatisfied with the IPC's unwillingness to negotiate on Iraq's terms, the Iraqi government gave the IPC an ultimatum with similar demands in May 1972. The IPC tried to offer a compromise solution but the Ba'athist government rejected the offer and, on June 1, 1972, nationalized IPC operations, which were taken over by the Iraq National Oil Company.

Wikipedia ibid.

Here we see the Baathist Party nationalize Iraqi petroleum in 1971. Iraq's oil would remain in the hands of the Iraqis until the war between the Americans and the Iraqis would result in the oil no longer being nationalized. By 2010 it was owned by Exxon, Shell, Occidental, etc.

There were a few contracts in 2018 with state owned oil companies, but they were not owned by Iraq.

In the Gulf War the American Army massed soldiers in Saudi Arabia to stop Iraq's Saddam Hussein, who the bourgeois called a bloody murderer as he tried to gain control of Kuwait's petroleum. The Baathist from the same party that had nationalized the oil just two decades ago had invaded Kuwait, a small rich monarchy under the Crown Prince Al Sabah, with much oil. Saudi Arabia, who had large military contracts with the American army, would allow the Army on their soil, to return Kuwait to monarchy, like Saudi Arabia.

It was quite a spectacle, and raged on and off for about 25 years; first Hussein was able to keep power, and the oil, only to be conquered and put to death by George II. George Bush 1 started the war to protect the Crown Prince Al Sabah, George II continued in his dad's tradition and finished off nationalized oil and Hussein. It was quite the bloody spectacle, and whole lives were spent trying to obtain control of a desert country with little resources besides petroleum under the ground.

By 2017 the oil was no longer nationalized by the Iraqis. The Iraq National Petroleum Company had been broken up, and it was now almost all large companies from the western nations in control of Iraq's oil.

It is not clear if this was the entire reason for American military activity, to gain control of the oil, but as rebuilding Iraq, totally destroyed after several wars, would almost entirely have to be rebuilt by America, the only way to make a profit was too sell the petroleum. At this point the Americans begin to see petroleum, which was causing climate change, as being the only way to profit from the Iraq adventure. They begin to disavow climate change and agreements in favor of maximum production by capitalists of the oil industry.

The bourgeois directly supported the overthrow of Saddam Hussein, who tried to nationalize Kuwait's petroleum. America first attempted to control the Iraqi's oil in 92' under George I and as they could not finish the job later invaded again under the next Bush (George II) in 2001, which was successful at securing the oil fields. The war then became a war with Islamic State. War in Iraq raged 16 years or so. After Afghanistan, which is on year 17, it was America's longest war in history, longer than Vietnam. With the popular government of Maqtada Sadr now in power nationalized oil could again become an issue, as the leader is more friendly to the Iraqi Communist Party.

Petroleum is causing climate change. It is now being mined by injecting Benzene into Shale deposits underground, Fracking. Benzene causes cancer, and it is not clear if it is ever going to come up after being injected in the ground. Nevertheless it has drastically lowered the price of oil, and this makes the quest for oil in Iraq and Iran less important for America. The Oil Sands projects in Alberta Canada also have been able to satisfy some of America's need for petroleum, further reducing reliance on Persian and Iraqi oil.

The Fall of Islamic State

The war against Islamic State in Iraq rather unceremoniously came to an end in 2017, with the surrender of the fighters there. Syria raged on into 2018, but for the most part the battle against Islamic State there was settled by 2018, with only a few small desert areas still under Islamic state control.

The northern part of Iraq is totally destroyed, with estimates of hundreds of billion of dollars worth of damages from American and Islamic state bombing. In Syria the conditions are similar; total destruction of several cities.

Islamic State was something that was sort of a self-fulfilling prophecy; America said Al Qaeda was in Iraq and went to war there. The little Bush somehow tried to connect Iraq to the World Trade Tower bombing, which was done by Afghanistan not Iraq.

Congress weighed in on this, and said there was no connection between 9/11 terrorism and Iraq. Al Qaeda sort of just sprung up once bombing of Iraq to remove Saddam Hussein started, whom the first George Bush was unable to remove with the first Iraq war.

So if America had left Saddam Hussein in power, would al Qaeda have taken over, and turned into Islamic State?

Syria's civil war started with the Arab Spring movement, which seems to have been rebellion against non-monarchy governments, heavily influenced by al Jazeera propaganda from Qatar, a country with feudalism. It was strange as no monarchies were targeted for universal suffrage, only countries where there was no Crown Prince would participate in the Arab Spring. The only exception was Bahrain, where rebellion was quelled as of late with Saudi Arabian help to support the Kalifa monarchy.

Syria received help from capitalist Russia, Iran and Lebanon's Hezbollah movement to defeat what became Islamic State. Russian aerial bombing seems to have kept Bashar Assad in power. As in Iraq, it was a bloody episode.

Islamic State seems to be gone, but where is the money going to come from to rebuild? Donald Trump may have to pay tens of billions of dollars to rebuild Iraq, which he has refused to use the state to do, and the petroleum is damaging the ecology with climate change. Even if they pump like there is no tomorrow, the effects are detrimental.

Once war started in Iraq it caused exactly what Bush said would occur, America would fight Al Qaeda. But there was no al Qaeda to start with when war was made on Iraq. A self-fulfilling prophecy...

In Syria, Iran and Hezbollah are in power, and the anti Semitism is growing. As of late no favor was done to Israel by the bourgeois recognizing Jerusalem as the Israeli capital. Israel may have a claim to Jerusalem, but Donald Trump was condemned for anti Semitism by the United Nations as he has and continues saying there are some anti Semitists who go to demonstrations in places like Charlottesville that are good people. That "our beautiful monuments" to white slavery should stay up. Yet Benjamin Netanyahu does not see the contradiction and supports Donald Trump.

It seems that if the Jewish people could not go to Israel they would have to come to America, like they did by the millions in the 19th century. Considering the verdict the Jews were black people, an idea supported by the Fascists, many bourgeois simply want to keep Europe and America white by having the Jewish in the desert in Israel instead of western countries. Anti Semitism exists in America too, and Donald Trump is viewed favorably now by many white supremacists. Israel keeps the Jews from immigrating to America, they go there instead. This may be why America is recognizing Jerusalem and Israel's 1967 claims as legitimate, and moving the Embassy to Jerusalem, it is racially motivated.

July- August 2018

Modern British Political Economic Conditions

Here we have what the House of Lords represents, hereditary peers with titles to land ownership. They are holders of titles which are sanctioned by the Queen, who is the leader of the nobility. Here we have what is remaining of feudalism in the west, as opposed to the east and the old Asiatic societies.

"Unlike the elected House of Commons, all members of the House of Lords (excluding 90 hereditary peers elected among themselves and two peers who are ex officio members) are appointed. The membership of the House of Lords is drawn from the peerage and is made up of Lords Spiritual and Lords Temporal. The Lords Spiritual are 26 bishops in the established Church of England. Of the Lords Temporal, the majority are life peers who are appointed by the monarch on the advice of the Prime Minister, or on the advice of the House of Lords Appointments Commission. However, they also include some hereditary peers including four dukes.

"The House of Lords scrutinises bills that have been approved by the House of Commons. It regularly reviews and amends Bills from the Commons. While it is unable to prevent Bills passing into law, except in certain limited circumstances, it can delay Bills and force the Commons to reconsider their decisions. In this capacity, the House of Lords acts as a check on the House of Commons that is independent from the electoral process.

"The House of Lords developed from the "Great Council" (Magnum Concilium) that advised the King during medieval times. This royal council came to be composed of ecclesiastics, noblemen, and representatives of the counties of England and Wales (afterwards, representatives of the boroughs as well). The first English Parliament is often considered to be the "Model Parliament" (held in 1295), which included archbishops, bishops, abbots, earls, barons, and representatives of the shires and boroughs of it."

Wikipedia House of Lords

The titles to social positions determining class and the relationship towards the rest of the society resembles Saudi Arabia, although of late it is waning in power. Still it is the workers who produce the wealth by labour, but are ruled by a person whose position is determined purely by birth, as a noble. The monarchy is in charge of the nobility whose hereditary titles occupy the House of Lords. Patriarchal arrangements of land ownership, without universal suffrage is the real origin of the

House of Lords. Like the monarchy it is part of another more simple time in British history, when the Queen was the head of the church, and insulting her was insulting God when the divine right of Kings reigned.

The Guilds, with Master, Journeyman, and Apprentice were the titles ascribed to the labourers of the Middle Ages. The master carried rank higher than labourer, and was a member of the Guild. A person could only be a member of the Guild if they had attained Master status, but were still under the nobility. In the Medieval cities the freemen would be just starting to assert dominance over the nobles in the Middle Ages, but the latter would reign unrestricted for several centuries after the first English Parliament. It is not until the mid millennia that the rising power of the bourgeois would significantly alter the House of Lords, albeit briefly.

"The power of the nobility declined during the civil wars of the late 15th century, known as the Wars of the Roses. Much of the nobility was killed on the battlefield or executed for participation in the war, and many aristocratic estates were lost to the Crown. Moreover, feudalism was dying, and the feudal armies controlled by the barons became obsolete. Henry VII (1485–1509) clearly established the supremacy of the monarch, symbolised by the "Crown Imperial". The domination of the Sovereign continued to grow during the reigns of the Tudor monarchs in the 16th century. The Crown was at the height of its power during the reign of Henry VIII (1509–1547).

"The House of Lords remained more powerful than the House of Commons, but the Lower House continued to grow in influence, reaching a zenith in relation to the House of Lords during the middle 17th century. Conflicts between the King and the Parliament (for the most part, the House of Commons) ultimately led to the English Civil War during the 1640s. In 1649, after the defeat and execution of King Charles I, the Commonwealth of England was declared, but the nation was effectively under the overall control of Oliver Cromwell, Lord Protector of England, Scotland and Ireland.

"The House of Lords was reduced to a largely powerless body, with Cromwell and his supporters in the Commons dominating the Government. On 19 March 1649, the House of Lords was abolished by an Act of Parliament, which declared that "The Commons of England [find] by too long experience that the House of Lords is useless and dangerous to the people of England."The House of Lords did not assemble again until the Convention Parliament met in 1660 and the monarchy was restored. It returned to its former position as the more powerful chamber of Parliament—a position it would occupy until the 19th century.

Wikipedia House of Lords

Oliver Cromwell was a military leader of the growing bourgeois, who had yet to conquer and subjugate the economic structure of society to capitalism. He did remove King Charles I, a revolutionary moment. But he thought he was guided by Christ, and was a pious Christian. The Royalists were the power behind the House of Lords, the nobility dominating debate. They were removed temporarily, but would return later.

Oliver Cromwell's bones would be dug up, and his body desecrated by the Royalists, who returned to power in 1660 under Charles II.

In the 19th century the House of Lords began to become less powerful than the House of Commons. But this did not mean there was popular representation in the House of Commons. It just meant the lower house was becoming more powerful.

Into the 20th century the House of Lords continued to exist.

"The Parliament Act 1911 effectively abolished the power of the House of Lords to reject legislation, or to amend it in a way unacceptable to the House of Commons: most bills could be delayed for no more than three parliamentary sessions or two calendar years. It was not meant to be a permanent solution; more comprehensive reforms were planned. Neither party, however, pursued the matter with much enthusiasm, and the House of Lords remained primarily hereditary. In 1949, the Parliament Act reduced the delaying power of the House of Lords further to two sessions or one year.

"In 1958, the predominantly hereditary nature of the House of Lords was changed by the Life Peerages Act 1958, which authorised the creation of life baronies, with no numerical limits. The number of Life Peers then gradually increased, though not at a constant rate.

"The Labour Party had for most of the 20th century a commitment, based on the party's historic opposition to class privilege, to abolish the House of Lords, or at least expel the hereditary element.

Wikipedia ibid

Modern Political Economic Conditions by Nicholas Jay Boyes

The House of Lords would be in power for about 700 years prior to the new millennium. It still exists, and has of yet to be made to have universal suffrage to appoint its members. Clearly it is also not dominated by worker parties either. The Labour Party became farcical after the attempt to exit the European Union, when they sided with the House of Lords position on exiting the single market.

"The Labour Party included in its 1997 general election Manifesto a commitment to remove the hereditary peerage from the House of Lords. Their subsequent election victory in 1997 under Tony Blair led to the (limited reform) of the traditional House of Lords. The Labour Government introduced legislation to expel all hereditary peers from the Upper House as a first step in Lords reform. As a part of a compromise, however, it agreed to permit 92 hereditary peers to remain until the reforms were complete. Thus all but 92 hereditary peers were expelled under the House of Lords Act 1999..., making the House of Lords predominantly an appointed house.

"Since 1999, however, no further reform has taken place. The Wakeham Commission proposed introducing a 20% elected element to the Lords, but this plan was widely criticised. A Joint Committee was established in 2001 to resolve the issue, but it reached no conclusion and instead gave Parliament seven options to choose from (fully appointed, 20% elected, 40% elected, 50% elected, 60% elected, 80%, and fully elected). In a confusing series of votes in February 2003, all of these options were defeated, although the 80% elected option fell by just three votes in the Commons.

Wikipedia ibid

The hereditary peers, representatives of the nobility, are still present. At best the Upper House is more appointed by the Prime Ministers Party than before. It remains to be seen when the temporary reforms as regards the hereditary titles amount to anything, given the Labour Party position on leaving the European Union and the fact they are represented now in the House of Lords who agree with Labour there should be a referendum again to determine if the British People no longer support exiting the European Union.

For 14 times now the nobility has opposed Brexit, constantly sending back legislation to leave the single market. The monarchy controls 92 nobles with titles in the House of Lords, Baron, Lords, and Earls etc., titles to hereditary privilege inherited from the middle ages. There are many intelligent people who believe the monarchy in Britain is purely symbolic. But the House of Lords is not symbolic, and has been trying to stop Britain exiting the single market after the universal suffrage produced a majority of British citizens who wanted out of the single market.

"... the government has been defeated 14 times in the House of Lords on the EU Withdrawal Bill.

"The House of Lords takes its role as a revising *chamber seriously. Peers like to think it is their job to warn the Commons to think again if they think the national interest demands it.*

"Specifically, that is the view of Angela Smith, the Labour leader in the Lords, and of her frontbench colleagues. Which is important, because they are semi-independent of Jeremy Corbyn. The Labour lords are more anti-Brexit than the Labour leadership in the Commons.

Independent May 9 2018

The Labour party holds seats in the House of Lords, and the holders of titles are still trying to keep Britain from leaving the European Union. In the European Union the leadership always suggests leaving the EU is reactionary, and the bourgeois there keep trying to suggest Britain is being manipulated by these reactionaries in leaving the single market. As if the single market is not something the reactionary bourgeoisie are in favor of. It is more of a threat really, that if the workers want to leave the EU their society will become like Germany in the 20th century when Hitler tried in vain to stop revolutionary workers movements. It is sort of an implicit threat, that they will have fascists joining the Communist Party in rejecting single market capitalism. The idea the reactionaries are against capitalism neglects to recognize their real views, and is a form of historical revisionism. The reactionaries like Mussolini and Franco were monarchy supporters, and it is no accident the Queen and her House of Lords support the market. It is one step closer to remaining in power as regards what happened to feudalism in most of Europe, when first the French revolution then the Communist revolutions swept out the royalists. In both cases the royalty has yet to reemerge, although it still might in Eastern Europe in this period of reaction.

"Sadiq Khan (Labour party mayor of London ed.) has set out the possibility of Britain remaining within the EU, arguing that Brexit could be legitimately stopped if the Labour party included the pledge in an election manifesto or committed to a second referendum.

Modern Political Economic Conditions by Nicholas Jay Boyes

"In a considered and powerful intervention that could raise the hopes of remain supporters, the London mayor described himself as "an optimist" about the possibility of the UK staying part of the European Union.

"But he said it was only possible to "trump the referendum" of 2016 in which 52% opted to leave the EU with a fresh, democratic vote, which could be delivered through the next general election or a national vote on the final Brexit deal.

7 17 2018 the Guardian

So here we have the party opposed to the House of Lords agreeing with them on Brexit.

Some opposition. After 14 attempts to stop Brexit by the monarchy, Labour is not complaining about hereditary seats and titles to land ownership any more. Instead they are supporting the House of Lords system, who have been constantly trying to put down the movement against the single market decided by universal suffrage.

A toothless opposition. Given it was the labourers who voted for the Brexit, the English proletariat outnumbers the bourgeoisie 10 to 1, the outcome is now subject to the nobles House of Lords government, the same government Labour used to be against they are now supporting. The Queens nobles just keep sending bill after bill back to the House of Commons to detooth Brexit.

"Support for Britain to remain in the EU single market and customs union is overwhelming among Labour party members, according to a poll showing that more than eight out of 10 think the UK should stay in Europe's key trading blocs.

Guardian 8 17 2017

It seems to be a contradiction; on one hand we have a party nominally a workers party, on the other hand we have a party supported by the House of Lords. Either someone is not telling the truth or we are having a hard time understanding what liberal democracy is producing in Britain…

"Former British prime minister Tony Blair told voters on Thursday that time was running out to reverse Brexit, a folly that he said would torpedo Britain's remaining clout and be regretted for generations to come.

""We are making an error the contemporary world cannot understand and the generations of the future will not forgive," Blair said in an article published on his website on Thursday.

"2018 will be the last chance to secure a say on whether the new relationship proposed with Europe is better than the existing one," Blair, 64, said.

Reuters 1 3 2018

But wait… Tony Blair enacted legislation to curb the power of the Lords, according too Wikipedia (see above). He tried to say that hereditary titles to government were wrong. they did not agree with the decisions of the Lords, and their power had to be curtailed. What is the current message?

Total U Turn Tony. Now he is left supporting the House of Lords against Brexit.

You can't have your cake and eat it too. At some point someone is going to have to nail down just what exactly the Labour Party feels about the Queen and her nobles, represented by the House of Lords.

Its been several years now and even after more than a dozen attempts by the nobility led by the Queen to stop Brexit it is still looking like there may be real change in Britain soon. Will the Labour Party be comfortable with the verdict history will be giving them, that on one hand they are rebels of some sort against the nobility, on the other hand they support bourgeois notions of single markets supported in the House of Lords?

The Labour party has representation in the House of Lords, something the socialists do not. The socialists in Britain have been fighting the House of Lords for more than a century, and make no concessions to the appointed and hereditary lords. They want the House of Lords gone completely, along with the single market Labour Lords. The Labour Party wants too keep having referendum after referendum until they have victory in keeping Britain in the single market. If the bourgeois they didn't want the opinion of the British worker, they should not have asked it. To be fair it was the Tories who asked for the suffrage about the European Union membership; Labour seems to be currently against it, as they want a rerun. A strange turn of events, like Churchill, conservative, supporting the Soviet Union, and even taking Britain to war in favor of it, an example of bourgeois support to revolutionary movements.

Modern Political Economic Conditions by Nicholas Jay Boyes

The British won the last time, and Churchill would be remembered in history as having put down the reactionary bourgeoisie in Germany and Italy. America even supported the British position during the war, although they would support the most repressive forms of capitalism later, with nuclear weapons designed to fight the Nazis directed at Soviet Union, to support the exploitation of the worker as wage labour.

July – August 2018

Ecology

Petroleum and Climate Change

It seemed not clear why Donald Trump would risk isolation as being the only country in the world not to have ratified the Paris Climate Change Agreements. Why would the appointed president of the United States not do a simple thing like reduce Carbon Dioxide produced by American industry, when the science clearly shows fossil fuel usage is causing climate change?

At a glance he said it would harm American capitalist industry. True, but we had gotten them to do recycling, and that was far more dangerous for capitalists as it was labour that carried no exchange value. Noone was paid to recycle or fined for not recycling. That is not capitalism.

So why then? Why not just go the route of America's neighbors and provide renewable energy to America?

Capitalist industry is capable of building and running solar and wind power. At worst for them they use state money to get started. But the state is used for many projects under capitalism, roads, trains, canals, etc. They use the state's money because capitalism needs a road, but cannot build it profitably. So they build it with the state.

In this case capitalism needed energy. Wind and solar were now cheaper to build than coal, or nuclear. Many of the larger renewable energy projects were already owned by capitalists, and they were making a profit.

So why not go this route? Why change directions?

America had just fought Iraq, and had been trying to colonize Baghdad for decades. They recently conquered Islamic State there. It was looking more and more like the bourgeois had secured control of some of the largest petroleum fields in the world. And they had removed the nationalized Iraq National Petroleum Saddam Hussein had tried to nationalize Kuwait's petroleum with.

Modern Political Economic Conditions by Nicholas Jay Boyes

It was just too good to pass up. Finally a profit coming from capitalist control of Iraq's petroleum, sold off to bourgeois buyers like Exxon Mobil and Chevron.

But there were new problems. Fossil Fuels were proven to be raising the temperature, with ecological consequences. Would the bourgeoisie be denied their prize, and seemingly endless supply of petroleum?

They were denied by the Paris Climate Agreements, brought to us by the French Democratic Socialists who organized the international treaty. It was a rejection of fossil fuels, the same fossil fuels that would have made Iraq a profitable adventure. Thus Donald Trump refused to ratify the Paris Climate treaty his predecessor Barack Obama had agreed too, by pulling out of the climate change agreements altogether.

It is not clear if petroleum was the whole reason to invade Iraq. We may never know that for sure, but it was their largest industry and whether or not that was the reason, it was definitely the only way of paying for rebuilding Iraq, whose cities were totally destroyed by decades of aerial bombing, in the first and second Iraq wars.

If you could not sell the oil, there was only desert soil left.

The American bourgeois were denied their prize. The petroleum was no longer an asset. The only thing to do was to reject the Paris Climate Change Agreements and risk isolation by not remaining part of it. Control the petroleum, and to hell with international agreements about problems with climate change. That is why capitalists could not abide by the Treaty, and Donald Trump represents American capitalists.

Regardless of the direction of America, there was a consensus fossil fuels were coming to an end. All the oil under Iraq would not change that. The Hurricanes were getting worse, winter was far milder, and drought was becoming more common. Climate change was real, and was caused by the fossil fuel under Iraq being burned. It was becoming a crutch of industrial development to use petroleum. Its days were numbered.

July- August 2018

American Isolationism and Economic Conditions

Isolation from the outside world and continuing economic decline has placed America in competition with India and China. The days of being able to compete with Western Europe are fading quickly. America is still not metric, the last country in the world not to switch to a more scientific system of measure. Do they even produce parts that are not metric anywhere other than America? Are there other countries who welcome American industry being sold they cannot build parts for as they are metric and American machinery is not?

As regards the Paris Climate Change Agreement, America is the only nation in the world that would not sign the agreement. Donald Trump said India and China were too competitive with American industry, and America would stay on fossil fuels until they run out. Further examples of America isolated and not getting along with its neighboring countries, in this case across the Atlantic in France. It is the western edge of Europe, not Poland. It is sort of on the border, like England. This also shows how weak American industry has become; they expect to be treated like India and China in the Paris Climate Change Agreements. If they were more industrially powerful they would not have to worry about the developing world being able to produce commodities cheaper and of higher quality than American commodities.

It all adds up to an isolated country unable to have a peaceful relationship with its neighbors, for instance the United Nations recently condemned the Embargo against Cuba, and every country in the world except America and Israel voted to end the embargo in the General Assembly. These types of things are becoming ever more common with Donald Trump.

On the COP 21 Agreements and Ecology

A historic moment occurred April 22 2016, when the leaders of the world's nations put aside their differences and for the sake of the ecology agreed to limit greenhouse gas emissions from industry.

China and India were not signatories to the previous attempt to create an ecology agreement, the Kyoto accords. America refused to sign the deal too due to this; they felt they were unfairly treated as India and China were allowed to burn more fossil fuels than America. This was due to the fact they are still the developing world, there were lower standards to achieve progress at ending fossil fuel consumption due to their material conditions.

Europe did not seem to mind, and signed the Kyoto Accords regardless of China and India's absence. They were not worried about competition from China and India, they were industrially advanced enough this did not trouble them. America, on the other hand, was in competition with metric India and China, and felt they could not compete with limits on how much fossil fuels they could use.

All nations of the world signed on to the Paris Climate Change Agreement, the next treaty, and pledged jointly to limit man made warming of the ecology to 1.5 degrees Celsius this century. Barack Obama supported the efforts to limit Climate Change; it was not until Donald Trump was appointed president America would drop out of the agreements.

The reason for this became clear when Iraq was conquered again, and the western petroleum industry removed nationalized oil in Iraq. The companies pumping the oil were private property, and about the only industry that was functioning enough to export. Even what modest agriculture was left in the north had suffered, and there were whole cites displaced. The oil was to be used to make the adventure to conquer Iraq profitable, rather than leaving the petroleum in the hands of the Iraqi people, as property of the nation.

It would seem to have been why Donald Trump would endure isolation, and find himself at odds with the scientific community whose research had shown climate change was real, by removing America from the climate change agreements. The climate change had been known for years, and the strange severe weather was only getting worse. The satellites were picturing the arctic poles losing glaciers, and the consensus was fossil fuel industry was to blame. No matter, Donald Trump just declared he did not believe the scientists and decided profits from the capitalists in

Iraq were more important than ecology. Without the profits Iraq would be a failure, an expensive show of American military strength that resulted in total destruction of Central and Northern Iraq, a weakened America, and a leader who still refuses to use state money to rebuild Iraq.

When Barack Obama agreed to try to stop fossil fuels, and join the climate change agreements with the rest of the world it looked promising. America was completely attached to fossil fuels, Coal was massively burned for electricity, petroleum provided energy for the cars, buses, railroads.... What Donald Trump did was something that can only be called protectionist, using state power to help the fossil fuel industries that were most effected by attempts to stop the burning of these energy sources.

His protectionism was also on display when he began removing state money that was helping solar and wind electricity production, and favored the coal industry. He went further to tariff imports of steel from Europe and Canada, the two main exporters of steel to America. The Integrated Mills were the target; the Electric Arc furnaces were already competitive in the world market. Integrated Mills produced about a third of American steel, and the Coal industry was using the coal product Coke to produce it.

"In 2017, there were 9 operating integrated steel mills in the United States (plus one idled), down from 13 in 2000. Integrated mills produced 31% of the steel produced in the US. In an integrated steel mill, iron ore is reduced to metallic iron. In the US, this is done in blast furnaces.

Wikipedia

The old mills, mostly non metric, were shut down or on the edge of failure. The tariffs were supposed to make industry produce commodities in America. Then first it was Harley Davidson, who announced that due to the tariffs, which raised the price of a Harley Davidson motorcycle $2,200 in Europe, Harley decided to produce parts in Thailand instead of America, where the tariffs would not effect production. This was the stated goal of Harley Davidson's owners, that the tariffs were not helping American industry. The steel mills may have been helped, but the protectionist tariffs were moving industry out of America. It was the president picking out who would materially benefit from supporting his bourgeois, and the fossil fuel industries supported his appointment as president. The climate change agreements directly challenged the industry, whose off shore drilling was controversial, as well as the greenhouse effect it was causing to consume their product. Donald Trump first and foremost protected the fossil fuel industry, like the Koch brothers who bankrolled his campaign to be appointed president, wealthy men who made fortunes selling petroleum products. Their money was spent to promote Donald Trump, and they owned the second largest company in America. The president did not get small contributions to get his seat, rather he was helped by the bourgeois as a member of their class. Their membership supported the president and in order to remain a Republican in 2018 you had to toe the line.

It should be remembered it was the capitalists whose fossil fuel industry caused most of the climate change. China was sort of revolutionary, but had a stock exchange and billionaires by 2010. The Soviet Union was no more, and socialism in Europe was gone. It was capitalism that caused the increase in warming, and the opponents of climate change were often socialists, although not the anthropocentric 20th century brand. It was not making a profit that brought us the Climate Change Agreements, it was the efforts by independent ecological worker groups with no economic incentive whatsoever just the idea of ecological change. Donald Trump was a perfect example of the bourgeois mind, capitalism first, ecology last. Create exchange value in all labour, trade the ecology for short term capitalist gain.

July - August 2018

Protectionism and Climate Change

In July 2017 the president went to Germany for the Group of 20 trade talks, and amid chaos on the streets proceeded to pull America out of the Paris Climate Change Agreements. He was starting to get ready to do protectionist trade practices as regards American Steel production.

For many years the Integrated Steel Mills had been unable to compete in the world market, they could not make a profit. They were distinct from Electric Arc Furnaces in that they used iron ore mined from the earth to create ingots. The Electric Arc furnace used scrap and recycled steel to smelt into ingots, it was not so reliant on virgin Iron Ores. The Integrated mills were often bailed out, the state lending money, etc.

It was part of a pattern by the appointed leader Donald Trump. His opposition to the Paris Climate Agreements and his protectionism of the Integrated Mills, the latter part of his fossil fuel industrial development, were connected. He pulled out of the climate agreements to favor Coal electrical production, and the Automobile Industry.

The auto industry was failing. General Motors and Chrysler were bailed out by Barack Obama, and have only recently became able to make a profit again. Ford announced they were only going to produce 2 kinds of cars in America, the Mustang, Focus brands and pickup trucks.

Nationalizing General Motors might have worked, but it carried a price tag of tens of billions of dollars. The industry was rapidly becoming obsolete, as electric autos were coming to dominate the market. Simply put, people did not always want big heavy fossil fuel using autos; they were expensive to fuel, as they are larger, and there is the real guilt of ecological consequences.

Ford Motors decided to produce only two kinds of cars in 2020 as 90% of its profits came from the pickup trucks it produced called the F Series.

General Motors is now private property, and Trump is trying to prop it up with the state again. His protectionism is rooted in maintaining outdated non metric industry, dirty and polluting. He also is protecting the Coal Industry, coal which is used for the Integrated Mills, known as Coke. Solvay Coke was in Milwaukee's port and after it closed, it sat for decades as it was too polluted to build on. It was only recently a large expensive project was undertaken to clean up Solvay Coke.

Modern Political Economic Conditions by Nicholas Jay Boyes

Electrical production is simply not cost effective when Coal or Nuclear Energy is used; they often were both present at the factory that produced electricity. Wind and Solar are becoming cheaper, and are less damaging to the ecology. Trump's protectionism was using the power of the state to make Coal profitable again. It was not exactly competition and free markets, rather Trump was allowed to pick and choose what people would become wealthy, and who would lose out by removing laws that protected society and ecology from pollution. They called laws "regulations" and proceeded to dismantle all laws that favored industry that did not use fossil fuels.

It looked like a losing battle. He must have known this.

America now stands alone against the Paris Climate Agreement.

Integrated Mills make up less than a third of American Steel production. One can only assume the other two thirds come from recycling and the Electric Arc Furnace.

July – August 2018

Climate Change and its Effects

A class 4 hurricane, named Harvey, recently made landfall on the coast of Texas, and weakened to a tropical storm above Houston.

Rainfalls of 75 Centimeters (30 inches) or more fell. Television from Houston showed massive flooding of urban and suburban neighborhoods under waist deep water.

Hurricanes occur when the ocean reaches temperatures of 82 degrees Fahrenheit (28 degrees Celsius) or more. The higher the temperature gets above 28 degrees Celsius, the more severe the hurricane gets.

Thus the obvious danger of the temperature raising a degree or two.

Houston is a large petroleum refining region. The Houston shipping canal between Galveston and Houston contains about half of America's oil refining. It flooded pretty bad.

At this point our bourgeois should have been reckoning if they still want to pull out of the Paris Climate Change Agreements. This was the first hurricane of the season. These types of storms could become a frequent occurrence if the ocean temperature continues to rise, which is obviously being caused by burning Houston's product, petroleum.

The climate change is the cause of this. Repeated dragging of the feet in regards to real commitments to reduce the use of petroleum by industry has caused this event.

Houston's downtown, skyscrapers and all, were all underwater as the Hurricane hit. This means the foundations were soaked, resulting in expensive repairs.

Hundreds of thousands of homes were flooded. Imagine the difficulty of moving a couch soaked with water out of the living room. It's hard enough to move a dry one. And what do you do with it after it is no good? Someone's ghetto landfill?

Will Houston try to get away from producing fossil fuels?

Unrest in Petroleum Producing Regions

There has been unrest in Venezuela as of late. President Maduro seems to have had American trade in much of the economy restricted or cut off. Interestingly enough though, petroleum, Venezuela's main source of income, its main export to America, was not cut off.

Apparently the bourgeois were worried about prices of petroleum in fossil fuel addicted America rising. As far as industrial countries go, America was more heavily sunk into oil than any other developed country into the 21st century. Without oil, much of America's industries wheels would stop stop turning.

Venezuela has been exporting to America for years. Hugo Chavez, who Nicolas Maduro replaced, was in charge of an empire exporting oil to America. It was what allowed for Chavez's democratic socialist experiment to be effective; at the time oil was worth twice as much prior to Hydraulic Fracking and Oil Sands production which lowered the price of oil, resulting in crisis in Venezuela and massive political unrest.

Without petroleum exports, Venezuela, already having a problem providing food and shelter to its workers due to low oil prices, became a disaster.

America also needed petroleum to continue its capitalist society. The petroleum industries all supported Donald Trump, who was appointed without the sanction of Universal Suffrage. The petroleum industries would do anything to continue to produce commodities with fossil fuels.

What President Maduro said, that Donald Trump, who lost the election by 3 million votes yet is still governing, having no moral authority to promote Universal Suffrage in Venezuela, is true. With the last Republican leader George II, who also did not have the sanction of Universal Suffrage, it was "Dictatorship or Democracy" in Iraq and Afghanistan. The contradiction should be self evident...

But in reality what this should show us is the need to stop relying on fossil fuels for America's energy needs. The instability in the petroleum producing countries should be enough to show that petroleum as a source of energy for industry is not the answer. It also is ecologically dangerous, it causes climate change.

It is sad to see Chavez's vision of a strong socialist Venezuela becoming less popular in the region. But land reform, breaking up of the Estates, which could have been a goal of Maduro and Chavez, unfortunately was not carried out. Thus the shortage of food, it was not like Cuba who broke up the large estates and gave the land to the workers to do small scale farming on, mostly for food. Venezuela, when the price of oil fell, began having trouble providing for its people, everything was invested in oil, oil for export. And the large estates were not nationalized, perhaps a revolution was required to allow for small scale land ownership, as it was no longer owned by small farmers, rather large agricultural companies.

It would seem to be the reliance on the export of petroleum that has weakened Venezuela. They were too sunk into fossil fuels, and could not change gears towards a more agrarian ecological society. Perhaps capitalism was too strong to allow for small farmers to work the land.

Socialism is not a dinner party. Real far reaching changes in society occur when the mechanism that creates surplus value, essentially profit, is altered. If the Communist Party takes power, the bourgeois will not purchase the oil. They will have to export it elsewhere. And even if they find a buyer there is no guarantee the price of oil will rise again.

The only way they will ever free themselves from capitalism is if they reject fossil fuels. But they have invested so heavily in fossil fuels they are totally dependent on export for even the most basic commodities. America will not fail even if the price of oil again rises, which would happen if Maduro could not export to America. The rise in oil prices might even not help him, as he could still not export to America, Maduro would have to look elsewhere to sell his oil commodity than America.

By August of 2018 Venezuela was a total wreck. They had been cut off financially and politically from the region. The currency failed, and had to be revalued, resulting in the money being now based on petroleum. It is very dangerous to have the money based on commodities that are essential to life. Gold and silver work precisely because they have little practical uses for industry that cannot be replaced with cheaper material if there is a supply problem. If the oil fails, the currency will also fail again. If gold is devalued it causes havoc, but it is still not essential for industry like steel, aluminum, oil. The money can be based on the price of oil, it is a commodity like the money. But given the demand for oil being met with Iraq pumping again, and capitalist western oil companies now doing the production as opposed to the nationalized oil production Iraq used to have, OPEC may have a hard time controlling the price of oil. A large part of the crisis in Venezuela is due to the price of oil falling due to increased production in America.

It was Venezuela's main industry, and its already failed once, and could happen again. If it does the currency will become devalued, and oil's value fell by almost half in the last decade. There is also the dream in the western world of someday being emancipated from fossil fuels by renewable energy. Owning what seems to be sort of a crutch, and speculating on it always being able to be needed could be a gamble.

Nuclear Energy and Lake Michigan

Nuclear energy is not an option for a replacement for fossil fuels.

Capitalism led to electrical production being done with fission. The constant drive to make bigger profits resulted in the exploitation of radioactive substances to boil water, the necessary key to producing electricity.

Now, decades after the construction of the first Nuclear Power production facilities, Lake Michigan's shoreline has been fouled by Waukegan's nuclear power company, for example. It sits dormant, its lifespan ended. It is now a monument to capital, a scar on the shore of the lake just a few kilometers south of Wisconsin border. And listen to the name they called it: "Zion Nuclear Power Plant". They had high hopes.

And people wondered why Chicago's bourgeoisie was not always welcomed in Milwaukee…

In Japan Fukushima's General Electric produced reactor melted down, and Waukegan was just lucky it did not fail as it was probably similar in construction. As of late General Electric is no longer listed in the Dow Industrials, its power fading and little hope of the people in Fukashima or Waukegan ever getting justice for ecological destruction.

Fukashima has cost Japan hundreds of billions of dollars, in pursuit of what was once called "energy to cheap to meter".

Waukegan is a sore. It is frightening how the drive for profit, with little or no thought about one's children and the world they have to live in, resulted in sacrifice of ecology for short term gain.

The admission that fission was a failure, and only good for war occurred to the Americans after they used it for war, but instead of rejecting fission they took a different route. So they had "Atoms For Peace" under Eisenhower, and they used fission to create electricity. They called it nuclear power, and it was viewed as a peaceful use of fission after the spread of nuclear weapons to a number of countries.

In Milwaukee today, nuclear power is not really used heavily. There may be a reactor providing a small amount of electricity near Kenosha in Illinois, but it is a small percentage of Milwaukee's consumption. Where there are still people reliant on nuclear reactors is Green Bay, Manitowoc, and Fond du lac. It is called Point Beach, and was designed to last 40 years in 1970.

This industry is very dangerous. There is radioactive discharge into Lake Michigan, the source of Milwaukee and Chicago's drinking water. It seems to be a small town industry, with Madison's bourgeois supporting the nuclear industry; Scott Walker has lengthened the life of the Point Beach reactors to 60 years.

The small towns seem to be sacrificing the health and ecological well being of the large cities for their capitalist manufacturing society.

Nuclear industry is clearly failing.

Building nuclear reactors is becoming more expensive than renewable energy. At least it was not as available as Wind and Solar energy was in the new millennium. The risk of meltdown, like General Electric's recent failure in Fukushima Japan, showed the failure of fission. Chernobyl also failed.

Time for the bourgeois to learn from their mistakes and face the historical reality, admit fission was a failure. Point Beach is threatening Milwaukee's clean water. Scott Walker's extending the lifetime of the reactors beyond what they were built for placed small town manufacturing ahead of the lives of millions of people at risk for a short term gain, profits.

Fission was a 20th century failure. It was useless as a weapon, it killed millions of civilians in Hiroshima and Nagasaki when Harry Truman used it there. The fission reactors are all at risk of a meltdown, and GE reactors are not much different in Point Beach as they are in Fukushima.

On the Decision to Build the Dakota Access Pipeline

In traditional American style, Donald Trump made a decision to finish building the Dakota access Pipeline through the Indian Reservations of South Dakota:

"The U.S. Army Corps of Engineers said it had granted ...an easement to Dakota Access LLC to allow the installation of a light crude oil pipeline under federal lands managed by the Corps at the Oahe Reservoir.

"The easement is the final permit needed for the controversial Dakota Access oil pipeline after an order from President Donald Trump to expedite the project despite opposition from Native American tribes and climate activists.

Reuters 2 28 2017

The Crow Creek Indians are a small group of Native Americans who live on the Missouri river system. They are directly affected by this. They were rather unceremoniously left there in the past by European settlers after the last of the northern tribes were conquered in South Dakota in the late 19th century.

South Dakota, the Black Hills, was promised to the Indians as their territory, but Manifest Destiny would guide the American bourgeois to place the entire territory of South Dakota under capitalist industrial development.

The Crow Creek Indians are cattle farmers, who once lived in the region by herding Bison. During the expression of Manifest Destiny the invading Americans attempted to extinct this species, as the Indians were totally reliant on Bison as a source of food.

Bison are a fraction of what they once were in South Dakota, there are fewer than several million wild Bison remain today compared to 60 million before the Americans expropriated the land from the peasants violently.

General Custer killed the last of the peasants who had been run up into the mountains, the Black Hills. The Black Hills today has no Indian Reservation. The remaining relatives of the peasants live in the desert adjacent to the Black Hills in the Pine Ridge Reservation and Crow Creek Reservation of South Dakota.

Modern Political Economic Conditions by Nicholas Jay Boyes

So the Indians are still on the reservations. Apparently they fear resistance if the peasants who once worked the land but were removed will rebel if allowed to again farm. There were many natives who fled their land to go west to make their last stand in South Dakota's Black Hills. Donald Trump took away their sovereignty on what is left of their land by putting the oil pipeline through, the Keystone XL. It's designed to move oil through and from North Dakota to Texas, as the Texans are protectionist and will not allow for the oil refinery to move north. The oil now has to flow south thousands of kilometers to be refined, then back up north thousands of kilometers, presumably in pipelines, in a refined condition.

It is a little rough in the South Dakota Reservations. They are good honest people, but there are problems with poverty as they have no industry, no Bison to herd, and the soil hardly even supports cattle on the Pine Ridge. The Badlands are part of the reservation, and are just this, Bad Lands.

America has always expropriated their land, and Donald Trump continues in a long tradition of the American bourgeoisie, slowly removing the last remnants of the Native American land from the people who discovered America, and lived in it for tens of thousands of year prior to the settlers arrival.

They are still alive, but their voices are rarely heard, and their numbers few. Needless to say they have little or no economic power, and are at the mercy of Donald Trump.

So in reality, nothing new happened when Donald Trump announced the oil pipeline was going through native lands. Americans have been removing the Native American peasants from their land for years, with "Treaties" or just straight up removal like the Mexican natives whose land the size of Western Europe was removed from them by war.

The American Dream of Manifest Destiny seems to require new settlements constantly, and this is only one more example of this.

The Internet and Marketing

Marketing and Society

Aggressive marketing tactics coming:

"The bill repeals regulations adopted in October by the Federal Communications Commission under the Obama administration requiring internet service providers to do more to protect customers' privacy than websites like Alphabet Inc's Google or Facebook Inc.

"The rules had not yet taken effect but would have required internet providers to obtain consumer consent before using precise geolocation, financial information, health information, children's information and web browsing history for advertising and marketing.

"The American Civil Liberties Union said last month Congress should have opposed "industry pressure to put profits over privacy" and added "most Americans believe that their sensitive internet information should be closely guarded."

Reuters

"Vinton Cerf, a co-inventor of the Internet Protocol and current vice president of Google, argues that the Internet was designed without any authorities controlling access to new content or new services. He concludes that the principles responsible for making the Internet such a success would be fundamentally undermined were broadband carriers given the ability to affect what people see and do online. Network neutrality is the principle that all Internet traffic should be treated equally. Internet traffic includes all of the different messages, files and data sent over the Internet, including, for example, emails, digital audio files, digital video files, etc. According to Columbia Law School professor Tim Wu, the best way to explain network neutrality is that a public information network will end up being most useful if all content, websites, and platforms (e.g., mobile devices, video game consoles, etc.) are treated equally.

"AT&T was... caught limiting access to FaceTime, so only those users who paid for AT&T's new shared data plans could access the application. In July 2017, Verizon Wireless was accused of throttling after users noticed that videos played on Netflix

and YouTube were slower than usual, though Verizon commented that it was conducting "network testing" and that net neutrality rules permit "reasonable network management practices"

Wikipedia Net Neutrality

This should show how capitalism marketing products is creating privacy concerns.

In its decision the FCC allows for Internet Providers, large companies run by capitalists, to use their ownership of the means of production to use personal web data to sell products to individuals.

It is scary because it gives them personal information like where you are and what you are doing, by tracking the GPS chip in your cell phone and could send you a message reminding you to buy a certain product, to send you a propaganda message, like McDonald's marketing to you a sandwich when you can smell the store.

In the quest of the bourgeois to sell their new charms, it would seem there are no holds barred. Any opportunity to make a profit will be taken, regardless of just how offensive their propaganda is.

It is funny, Americans had grown so used to marketing all capitalist owned media regularly interrupted broadcasts with propaganda. When the elections came it was a means of buying a seat. If you had the capital, your propaganda message was there on the television.

There was a time the worker was locked into advertising. When television and radio were king there was no way to get around advertising, and music was not free.

In today's world we have Netfix, You Tube, etc. There is little or no advertising, and it becomes quite obvious just how degraded our viewing habits had become due to marketing.

There is also the adblock technology available. It removes the offensive marketing, allowing for studying news without the propaganda. Its status is contentious,. The Washington Post and New York Times do not have to send the propaganda that comes whether or not you block it, they are paid for by subscription. They are also have some of the highest quality journalists in the country, the Washington Post last year won the Pulitzer Prize for its reporting on the Trump –Russian oligarch connections.

But what opposition to net neutrality really comes down to is capitalism, to be able to circulate commodities faster, in ever greater quantity. Capitalism is driven by a constant amount of new needs, and marketing is designed to make the worker consume commodities. Every producer of commodities wants workers to consume his product.

Of course, it is questionable if he wants his own workers to consume, as he pays them only enough to survive and continue labouring, and even getting enough money for union dues is a real political struggle for the labourer.

Nevertheless as long as capitalism exists there will always be a motive by capitalists to use any means possible to sell their new charms. Marketing allows for production to turn over its commodities faster, and make a profit easier. That is why it is so aggressive that even basic privacy protections are a barrier for capitalist production to overcome. Marketing is so intertwined with capitalism it is a fixture of modern society.

As material conditions change, capitalists are getting increasingly desperate to turn over their commodities. The new material conditions, computers, are a little harder to control. Marketing can be turned off, i.e. advertising blocking technology. It looks like the marketing bourgeois are still trying to use propaganda on their news outlets and entertainment online, but are slowly losing the battle, and want the user to have no choice but to see their propaganda messages anytime they connect to the internet. It's like saying because the Post Office carries your mail they have a right to read it and send you messages about it. They now resort to invasive marketing, using the internet service providers data, which was once private, to turn over commodities. Their days may be numbered. Not only is it stopping net neutrality unpopular, and required dictatorship to accomplish, it does not seem compatible with modern computer technology. Time will tell if marketing can survive in new material conditions of the age of computers.

July – August 2018

Politics in America

United Nations Condemnation of Anti-Semitism by Donald Trump's Government

The reactionary bourgeois and the resistance to them were visible in Charlottesville North Carolina at the demonstrations in 2017. Openly armed anti semitists showed up to fight against removal of a pro slavery monument to Robert E. Lee, who led the Confederate Army that fought for secession because they wanted black slavery. Donald Trump suggested not only that there were good white supremacists at the demonstrations, but that the resistance was also to blame for the bloodshed, when the reactionaries attacked unarmed workers demonstrating, by ramming a vehicle into them killing one and severely injuring dozens. To add insult to injury he stated publicly that he felt bad that "our beautiful Monuments were being taken down" as other states removed the secessionist symbols the reactionary supporters of Adolf Hitler had seized upon to justify anti Semitism. The connection with the European bourgeois reactionaries should be self-evident as they consider Jews to be black.

The United States got condemned by the United Nations thanks to Donald Trump:

"...a body of United Nations experts on Wednesday denounced "the failure at the highest political level of the United States of America to unequivocally reject and condemn" racist violence, saying it was "deeply concerned by the example this failure could set for the rest of the world."

"The committee (on Elimination of Racial Discrimination) called the Charlottesville violence, which took place mainly on Aug. 11 and 12, "horrifying" and said it was "alarmed by the racist demonstrations, with overtly racist slogans, chants and salutes by individuals belonging to groups of white nationalists, neo-Nazis, and the Ku Klux Klan, promoting white supremacy and inciting racial discrimination and hatred."

New York Times 8 23 2017

Donald Trump then attempts to show he has popular support for his bourgeois, but responds to the next peaceful demonstration with a large cloud of chemical irritants to disperse labourers gathered against anti Semitism at his event in Arizona.

"After a two-story cloud of gas rose over the streets for several blocks, protesters fled in every direction to escape the gas. Nonetheless, Harris said, none of the protesters he saw crossed the barrier lines established by police, instead running away from the convention center.

"At least a dozen protest groups had melded together outside the center in downtown Phoenix throughout the afternoon and evening under a common cause to oppose the president's policies.

AZCentral 8 2 2017

The United Nations condemnation showed the isolation of America regarding anti Semitism from the newly appointed government of Donald Trump.

Often the United States attempts to suggest the United Nations supports their use of violence in the developing world. Britain too, with the repeated statement by Tony Blair of a fictitious United Nations "mandate" to bomb Iraq. The United States also claimed United Nations support to bomb Iraq, which it also did not have. Kofi Annan, leader of the UN repeatedly called the Iraq war illegal, and refused to give United Nations support to it.

The United Nations was part of the post war order created by the Allied Powers after the Second World War. One of its goals was to make sure the Holocaust never occurred again.

Are we to really believe the United Nations does not know what anti Semitism is?

Responding to the Arizona protests with tear gas only reaffirmed Trump's bourgeois isolation from the outside world. The massive cloud of tear gas; the police arriving wearing gas masks… They were prepared to fire the chemicals to disperse the crowd. Where were the pictures of things being thrown at police? A smoke bomb provoked that? They came to fight the resistance, and they did, with tear gas and the club.

The dictatorship was condemned by the United Nations today for anti Semitism, and condoning violence against workers demonstrating against the reactionary bourgeoisie. The disproportionate threats and violence against the workers by Trump and his supporters were visible at the Charlottesville gathering, when they came armed with automatic weapons.

What Donald Trump Should Teach Us

The appointment of Donald Trump, his statements, and the decisions he has made as president are precisely the way we have been describing the economic structure of capitalism. His ascent to power; appointment without the sanction of universal suffrage, shows exactly what he is: a billionaire capitalist.

Of course, the bourgeois considered his experience as a financial capitalist to make up for his clear lack of political experience. This was seen as his ability to lead, he was in charge of money capital as a private property owner, selling properties he would acquire with his family's fortune. He was also a casino owner, trading money for money rather than producing a commodity, for instance like steel.

The closest thing to real commodity production he was involved in was expensive hotels and golf courses, luxury production.

It should come as no surprise his feelings about workers, for instance his statements about Charlottesville and the reactionary following he has. Donald Trump has not been rejected by his following for saying there were good white supremacists, if anything he was supported by the reaction. When it happens that it is objectionable to someone, it is his lack of political experience that has caused it, and it should be overlooked.

His use of social media, the two sentence Twitter responses, are his real bent. They come out daily, and are always against the press or the more moderate bourgeoisie, the Democrats, in particular the woman who he lost the election to, Hillary Clinton. He still attacks the first woman to ever win the sanction of universal suffrage in America, and perhaps in his twisted world he really believes he actually won the election.

Of course, no one else does. It is obvious he is a dictator. But that should come as no surprise as he is a billionaire capitalist. That is acceptable to his following, and it is the way capitalists function. His bombastic statements are what we have come to expect, and his laws he makes are a product of his businessman background.

Make no mistake; he does not represent the proletariat. When he passed his Tax laws, he said to the capitalists, "I just made you a whole lot richer". Whether he did or not remains to be seen. The Government does not willingly nationalize commodity producing industry capable of making a profit. If state industry can be run for a profit, it is, and it ceases to be owned by the state. So there comes a limit to how much taxes can really be cut, without being able to maintain essential industry for production that happens to not be able to currently produce a profit, but is needed for commodity production, i.e. highways, passenger trains, the bus, etc. These works are unable to create surplus value, but still needed by capitalists. That is why they exist, regardless of the fact they are not able to make a profit. Without them capitalism would not be able to function, the worker must be able to get to work, for example, so he can continue laboring thus capitalists need the bus and the highway. He also needs to be able to work, so he needs basic health care. Without healthy labourers it is impossible to make a profit. And of course there are things like in-state college tuition that have to be paid for as it creates middle class minds that are going to prove themselves and be allowed to join the bourgeois.

All the appointment of Donald Trump has done in a year is to reaffirm what we have always known to be the real feelings of the exploiting class towards their workers. Donald Trump is not an aberration from the feelings of the workers so called "betters". The Republicans all support Donald Trump in the Senate. When it comes time to appoint Supreme Court justices for life the Senate closes ranks, and all the bourgeois all support Trump. He is the leader of the Republican Party, and dissent in the ranks of the party a subject for dismissal.

Donald Trump has yet to break any new ground. He is no different than any other member of America's political class. All his appointment should show us is what we have always said billionaire businessman believe in was true. That they are only concerned with creation of a greater amount of relative surplus value. To that end it is no holds barred...

Stephen Bannon, who was involved in Trump's appointment, gave a speech today to the reactionary bourgeois National Front of Marine Le Pen. The party was headed by Marine's father, Mr. Le Pen until 2011 :

"Jean-Marie Le Pen, the former leader of France's far-right Front National, has once again been convicted of contesting crimes against humanity for saying the gas chambers used to kill Jews in the Holocaust were only a "detail" of history.

"A Paris court fined Le Pen €30,000 (£24,000) on Wednesday for the comments he reiterated on a French television programme in April last year.

"Le Pen, 87, had told the TV interviewer he had no regrets over calling the gas chambers a mere detail of the history of the Second World War, saying he stood by that view "because it's the truth".

Guardian 6 5 2016

National Front would nominally become the National Rally, but the National Rally was still led by his daughter Jean Marie Le Pen, and had the same old concepts.

So here we have a person who was a Trump administration member who is appealing to a fascist bourgeoisie. The Bannon connection follows Ms. Le Pen's niece speaking to a Donald Trump corporate conservative meeting, where her National Front membership was her credentials.

The exploiting class is moving closer and closer to the Western European reaction, as we see with Bannon addressing National Front Rallies. His latest project, suggesting that threatening to leave the European Union has reactionary support, is a farce. It's like giving the worker a choice between a middle of the road capitalist or someone extreme, and when they vote for the liberal suggest they have the real support of the worker. Bannon plays the reactionary role, a stick to the proletariat to support the capitalist leadership in Western Europe, or get a leader like Marine Le Pen.

Capital and its Owners

It is not so hard to understand who is really running the country:

"Seven Republican super-donors helped bankroll the conservative push for power in the 2016 election cycle, between them pumping more than $350m (£264m) into federal and state races."

"The Paradise Papers illuminate another aspect of these vastly wealthy men – their propensity to nurture offshore some of their combined fortunes, estimated by Forbes at $142bn...

"Warren Stephens, a major Republican donor, was the hidden co-owner of a payday lending company US authorities are suing for $50m after it allegedly used predatory tactics to deceive customers about the true cost of their loans.

"The Paradise Papers reveal that the billionaire financier (Warren Stephens), based in Arkansas, holds a 40% stake in the lender's parent company, which donated widely to US political campaigns over recent years while its link to Stephens was generally unknown.

"Charles and David Koch control Koch Industries, the second largest privately held company in the US. In 2005, they bought the paper and pulp giant Georgia-Pacific for $21bn.

"The Koch brothers have spent years building up a network of rightwing donors as an alternative power base to the Republican National Committee. In the 2016 presidential election, they invested about $250m trying to sway the US Senate and other contests, and have pledged to pump up to $400m into the midterms next year.

"Despite minimizing their tax contribution to government coffers, the brothers, each worth an estimated $49.2bn, project themselves as patriots and claim through their primary organising body, Americans for Prosperity, to be focused on increasing the wealth of all citizens.

"The casino magnate Sheldon Adelson gave $100m to Republican candidates in 2012, followed by $77.9m in 2016 and $5m to Trump's inaugural festivities, according to the Center for Responsive Politics. Information that Adelson has

already made public shows he runs three jets in Bermuda, including two Boeing 747s customized for luxury travel.

"The planes are operated alongside Adelson's fleet of 16 private jets in Las Vegas for the use of his company's executives and VIP guests.

"Adelson, 84, owes his estimated $35bn fortune to Las Vegas Sands, the casino empire he built and of which he remains chairman and chief executive. The company owns the Venetian Las Vegas hotel and casino.

"Geoff Palmer, 67, has an estimated personal fortune of $2.1bn. His homes include a $23.6m mansion in Beverly Hills and a $17.3m mountaintop house in Aspen, Colorado.

Geoff Palmer "described affordable housing quotas as "immoral", last year donated $5m to a Super Pac that supported Trump's presidential campaign and $310,000 to Trump's "victory fund". In 2012, he gave $500,000 to Romney's failed Republican presidential campaign.

"Steve Wynn, the Las Vegas and Macau casino mogul, became finance chair of the Republican National Committee in January...

The Guardian 11 7 2017
https://www.theguardian.com/news/2017/nov/07/us-republican-donors-offshore-paradise-papers

Clearly the shift away from universal suffrage has it roots here. This group of casino owners, usurers, and capitalists have been responsible for bankrolling what is the Republican Party suspension of the necessity of having popular support to govern.

They used material that people would identify with, based on facebook accounts with the Cambridge Analytica spying to have it look like it was some sort of rebellion that produced Donald Trump. By spying on facebook Stephen Bannon, who was a vice president of Cambridge Analytica, found phrases like Deep State, Fake News, Drain the Swamp, resonated with Americans. Facebook got used by Bannon and Trump as a staging ground for an American dictator to get appointed president, Donald Trump, just like George II.

Politics in America – Capital and its Owners

Universal suffrage in America has been permanently tarnished so this handful of wealthy people can continue making a profit. If universal suffrage does return to America it will only be the lower house of Congress that anyone takes seriously.

In the above article we see the economic structure of capitalism obviously in control of the political system. A small group of capitalists capable of control of massive wealth, and leveraging the political system to increase their control over the means of production.

What these papers show is not so much avoidance of taxes, but the exploitation of the worker. This money is capital; stored up labour power to control living labour. The sums are colossal, billions of dollars, and offshore accounts appear to be a way to keep the level of this exploitation of the worker by creating surplus value in production hidden. How much of this money is parked in small islands to keep it out of the view of the labour unions that represent the workers whose labour created this wealth?

Propaganda and Material Conditions of the Press

One can clearly see historical material conditions and the opinions of people when you look at how a person used to get news and how they do now.

I'm referring to the shift away from cable Television and radio to computers.

The news shows were mostly entertainment on the 5 o'clock news broadcast on the television station, but also carried propaganda messages called political advertisements.

They called this propaganda effort on television, radio, and paper newspapers "Political Action Committees" or PAC's. It was a very direct propaganda apparatus controlled by and paid for by capitalist money gained through exploitation of the labourer, and used to cement their control of their workers.

What was not so direct was we all had learned to tolerate the endless messages about capitalist industry, commercials, to promote the market. Viewers were expected to increase demand for capitalist produced cheap commodities due to the influence of propaganda.

No bourgeois controlled industries would send a revolutionary message.

Marketing is clearly a form of propaganda.

By 2010 computers could have the advertisements turned off with ad blocking technology. This was revolutionary, it removed the capitalist propaganda. It was still contentious at the time of writing, with attempts to beat the adblocker by capitalists to force their commodities on the consumer whether he liked it or not.

The internet allowed for the international press, for example Reuters or the BBC, to be accessible to anyone with a Personal Computer (PC).

Donald Trump and "Fake News"

President Trump has put down virtually all major newspapers and media that are the main sources for news online. The Washington Post, New York Times, CNN have all been labeled fake news by the appointed president. CNN was mostly cable news, but proved to be too much for the president, who watches this form of television. His following also watch cable news. The medium, complete with market propaganda, was still used for gathering news in the late 2010's, although mostly by the less literate who did not use computers, white males over 50 and veterans, Donald Trump's loyal following.

What people are supposed to be listening or viewing according to Trump seems is FOX News, and AM and FM radio. If it comes in as a radio signal, on the wave television set, or is a radio broadcast, it is safe. So are cable news stations that carry the bourgeois press. When a proletarian message sneaks through, it is simply labeled "fake news" by Donald Trump.

Who really cares about cable news anyways? The amount of time the leadership spends trying to control television broadcasts harken back to a simpler time. It was a time before the Internet, when news came from Channel 6, and you simply turned on the television set to watch it. His opposition to internet news sources is going to brew into a crisis at some point. Once the average American finds out they are being lied too on the radio, and that the Internet is a real source for the truth, we may see the end of commercial radio.

Crisis. The companies have their propaganda on the commercial radio and television. For years they had a system to not only justify their propaganda "advertisements", it paid for the television station to broadcast for free, it also provided the bourgeois with a market for their new charms and political messages supporting large capitalists.

It may be harder for capitalism to function in the world of ad block technology.

It is to his own undoing he calls the internet news sources "mainstream media" and "fake news". Companies like the New York Times and Washington Post have sunk capital onto the new method for reading the news. It would be hard for them, even if they wanted too, to reverse course and return to paper editions. Not only is it more costly, it causes ecological damage pulping, printing, bleaching etc

Donald Trump and Journalism

It's becoming more frightening to write about the political scene in Washington than ever. With the appointment of Donald Trump Twitter and FOX News have become the only press the president does not consider "fake news".

By ratcheting up the state apparatus to censor by press Trump dislikes, and continually casting doubt even on the sanity of journalists who report on him, what he calls the "Trump Derangement Syndrome", he is stirring up distrust of journalists. His attempts to censor the press, who he calls "unpatriotic" for doing their jobs by reporting on the president, seem to be having effects on the public.

"Speaking in front of U.S. military veterans before the 119th Veterans of Foreign Wars National Convention on Tuesday in Kansas City, Missouri, President Donald Trump made disparaging remarks when he called out "fake news" coverage of his trade agenda.

"Stick with us. Don't believe the crap you see from these people—the fake news," President Trump said. Several audience members turned towards the press pen, lobbing boos and hisses at members of the media as the remarks drew some of the biggest ovations during the president's speech, according to media reports.

"Just remember what you're seeing and what you're reading is not what's happening," Trump continued.

Newsweek 7 25 2018

These two events are connected; when you start demonizing the press, you stir reactions of the population against journalists.

A journalist's job is to cover the news, and they often put their lives in danger abroad and at home, opposing an irate president who has the ability to threaten journalists as "enemies of the people". The result of assuming the press of being "enemies of the people" results in violence against the press like Annapolis. It is becoming more dangerous with the reaction in power to speak the truth.

On June 28 2018 in Annapolis Maryland:

"A man armed with a shotgun and smoke grenades stormed into the newsroom of a community newspaper chain in Maryland's capital on Thursday afternoon, killing

Modern Political Economic Conditions by Nicholas Jay Boyes

five staff members, injuring two others and prompting law enforcement agencies across the country to provide protection at the headquarters of media organizations. The suspect, Jarrod W Ramos, 38, was taken into custody at the scene and was charged on Friday morning with five counts of first-degree murder.

New York Times June 2018

Here we have disrespect for the press playing out in the real world, not Trump's bubble in Washington. Real bloodshed, more similar to Honduras than America. It is coming with a general feeling of disrespect for journalists, that they are not telling the truth and are bad people.

Outside America, journalists often go to war zones to bring news to the country. Often it is slanted, but there is no way of knowing what is transpiring on the battlefield when the bourgeois send out the workers children to fight for them without the New York Times and the Washington Post. They may publish news with a capitalist bent, but they really do report from the fronts, as they are on the ground with the military and police.

Another danger is what other countries do when they see the bourgeois threatening the press as "fake news". It makes journalists lives more endangered, and emboldens censorship efforts outside and inside America. Press censorship is a real phenomenon, and Donald Trump is encouraging other capitalist leaders to use this method to cement control of the working class.

So why was Donald Trump constantly putting down the press?

Was the capitalist Washington Post and New York Times really to extreme for him?

The idea seems to have been to muscle the press, which was reliant on making a profit, to accept his economic ideas, which do not contain the words "capital" "Work Stoppage" "Surplus Value"...

Press censorship takes many forms. The Washington Post and New York Times may not always get the story right. But restricting the press, even the more tame press like these two newspapers, can only be called reactionary.

The press has a right to question the leadership of the government. In fact, it is their job to do this. There are times it is important to take in opposition opinions, and
78

even the large press sometimes publish stories critical of Donald Trump. Which of course was what the bourgeoisie is trying to stamp out.

Donald Trump was having success in controlling the press, Google News was one of the first to buckle. The Google News edition once carried news from Gramma International, the Cuban press. Today most of the time Google News is tabloid, or toes the capitalist line.

But should we be surprised at Google news, the same company who until recently was doing work for the state in Artificial Intelligence, the same state that hates independent worker organizations like the Communist Party? What did Google think it was being used for, tea and Crumpets?

Of late they have stopped providing official assistance to the military laboratories using the Artificial Intelligence to repress the proletariat. We can only assume they are no longer needed; that the military got what they needed to support capitalists violently from Google and no longer need their services.

So it should be no surprise Google news is propaganda now. Donald Trump claims another victory, censorship of the beginnings of a new type of free press, the aggregator of internet news.

Capital constantly strives for a breakdown of boundaries, and the soul of the human being is no barrier. Press censorship by a government without the sanction of universal suffrage looks more like martial law than liberal democracy. Google news is gone, and it is not coming back. Are we really to believe stories that it once brought us about Cuba are no longer popular? That no one really cares about the Cuban press?

July – August 2018

Rupert Murdoch and FOX Cable News

Media in American cable television is totally dominated by large capitalists. FOX News is owned by Rupert Murdoch, an Australian man who owns a number of news stations in the world, and in 1985, became a naturalized U.S. citizen.

His bourgeois political views have led him to support Margaret Thatcher, Tony Blair, and a number of politicians in America like Donald Trump.

"In July 2016, after the resignation of Roger Ailes due to accusations of sexual harassment, Murdoch was named the acting CEO of Fox News.

"Murdoch consolidated his UK printing operations in Wapping, causing bitter industrial disputes. His holding company News Corporation acquired Twentieth Century Fox (1985),HarperCollins (1989), and The Wall Street Journal (2007). Murdoch formed the British broadcaster BSkyB in 1990 and, during the 1990s, expanded into Asian networks and South American television. By 2000, Murdoch's News Corporation owned over 800 companies in more than 50 countries, with a net worth of over $5 billion.

Wikipedia Rupert Murdoch

He is now an American citizen, but his views more closely align with the colonial masters in Australia. It would seem Rupert Murdoch is more of a staunch British bourgeois, owning television stations that are competitive with the BBC like SKY, the former not owned by capitalists rather the state.

He is now in control of FOX, which is where the president expects workers to get their news from. He thinks everyone should be watching cable television, and paying for it. It costs about $100 a month for cable, and it is totally dominated by capitalist news companies like Rupert Murdoch's FOX News. There is rarely a revolutionary message on Cable television, and if there is it is considered an accident that costs someone their job.

The quantities of capital involved are intense. FOX News is worth a good billion dollars in capital. By allowing for marketing propaganda that regularly interrupts the broadcasts, Murdoch's company is profiting. They also do political propaganda, paid for media access to the highest bidder for a spot on FOX for profit.

Modern Political Economic Conditions by Nicholas Jay Boyes

This is not unusual for cable television stations, but considering it is becoming the presidents mouthpiece its bias towards capitalists like Trump who can pay for political messages must be noted.

Not to mention there are many workers who do not get paid enough to own cable television, and just use broadband for news.

Is the bourgeois trust put in Rupert Murdoch well placed? It is an American success story, he has been a citizen for 38 years now, and is a powerful man. But trust in an immigrant is not exactly something we have come to expect from Donald Trump. He distrusts the Canadians, America's closest neighbor, and has placed tariffs on steel and aluminum exports from Canada to America. He now places complete trust in an Australian bourgeois man?

It is a question of just what type of immigration the exploiting class wants. A working class man has a hard time getting citizenship if he is foreign. Given the distrust of Mexicans immigrating, and the unlikelihood of the migrant being anywhere near as wealthy as Rupert Murdoch at any time in his life, I guess Trump really likes Australians. Things like Kangaroos, Crocodile Dundee, cattle ranching come to mind. It is the other side of the planet, little is known about it.

Rupert Murdoch represents FOX News as he owns it. He is in control of a capitalist empire, and is the president's news source. Scrutiny of his real alliances is due. He must be loyal to Donald Trump, as they are close and both billionaires. Donald Trump really likes Australians and Cable television…

August – September 2018

Attempts by Capitalism to Overcome its Contradictions

It is interesting to see how capitalism attempts to correct problems that come to light, often contradictions that it has a hard time rectifying. The latest challenge to the bourgeois is the press questioning why they are being asked not to do their jobs, which include reporting on the president. To a man who wants workers to get their news from cable television, and constantly attacks the even the press that do this form of journalism, all we hear is complaints about how his group is being treated.

It seems like everyday we hear CNN and NBC being called "fake news" by Donald Trump. In response to the obvious concern he is censoring the press, or at least trying to (which is unlikely not to work as the press he is constantly whimpering about is owned by large scale capitalists), he responds that his bourgeoisie are being censored.

Every time capitalism is questioned Donald Trump says "I know you are but what am I". Capitalism attempts to overcome its contradictions, although it is never really capable of completely shaking off its problems, in this case the workers who support Trump and pay a hundred dollars a month for the cable television he is promoting realizing they get better news from the Internet, which is far cheaper and in text.

Of course his following, who are over 50 and veterans, when they see the contradictions, sometimes question things like why hundreds of press organizations across America rebuked Trump's attempts at censorship recently, including ecologicalera my website. Trump said "….Censorship is a very dangerous thing & absolutely impossible to police. If you are weeding out Fake News, there is nothing so Fake as CNN & MSNBC, & yet I do not ask…" etc.

So instead of directly answering the press, whose journalists are constantly being asked to censor their writings by Trump, he just points the finger at cable television stations that are too worker friendly for him. Capitalism trying to overcome the contradiction that in order to maintain its rule it has to lie, and promote illiterates watching television instead of reading and writing books and the internet. In that respect it is sort of pointless to argue with him as cable television seems to be going the same direction as AM radio, looking outdated.

Modern Political Economic Conditions by Nicholas Jay Boyes

The working class in America are among the worst repressed group of people in western society. Censorship is a human rights problem. It occurs when capitalism is under threat, as its illogical contradictions become visible. The zeal in doing things like censoring the press by the bourgeois, who seem to relish seeing Donald Trump up there encouraging ignorance, squarely places them in the category of tyrants. The only way to overcome the contradiction of the supposed strong arguments for capitalism is to discredit your opponent, calling the arguments of the workers "fake news", and cover up anything that does not agree with the opinions of the exploiting class, who know full well how scandalous it is to treat workers as wage labour.

Thus we can only call Donald Trump one of the more repressive western leaders, in what looks like the late stages of capitalist industrial development. The more he tries to discredit and suggest workers not read the media that has the nerve to question him just exposes the weakness of his bourgeois and their ideas. They are not even metric. Aside from a military of what was a front country against the working class, the opposition to socialist ideas formed what was a bulwark against Europe, there is just raw capitalism. When the arguments that supported this began to fail, America twice went to dictatorship, under George II and Donald Trump. The latter leader without the sanction of universal suffrage is attempting to censor the press.

It may have worked in the past, when television was the king of press. Paying for cable television was once universal, and the following of Donald Trump are from before computers came to dominate the press. They watch cable news, and are paid enough to afford the bill for it. The real opposition to Donald Trump is in print and primarily online. It is not the literate section of the proletariat supporting Trump, it is the reactionaries. There is a correlation between supporting the bourgeoisie and being illiterate. Donald Trump seems to have found this, and is exploiting it.

August – September 2018

American Political Conditions

It seemed like every day there was more knowledge of cooperation between the Eastern European capitalist states and the presidency of Donald Trump.

He made many statements denying cooperation with the Russians, which were proven wrong, most of the time by the New York Times and the Washington Post.

It came out the president's son attempted to have the Russian bourgeois help out his father defeat Hillary Clinton. First the New York Times found out about a meeting with a Russian bourgeois representative and Donald Trump Jr., Jared Kushner, and Mr. Manafort, members of Donald Trump's government. Donald Jr., fearing the press would print his emails, made them public.

Prior to getting caught, there was no mention of cooperation with Russian government to get Trump appointed. In fact, only angry denials anything of value was discussed. Later Trump would admit it was to get information about Hillary Clinton, the woman who won the sanction of universal suffrage only to be denied it by Trump.

It came out in August of 2018 Donald Trump admitted he wanted Russian assistance at the meeting.

The pattern of blatant lies, and plausible denials until caught, so common we learned not to trust anything the president or his government said. It all seemed like propaganda to stop European socialists.

There is one group of people who seem to not question Trump's statements, Russia Today. His most blatant lies about his collusion with the Russian bourgeois were reported as fact on Russia Today, that he had not had the above mentioned meeting, which he said was later was normal, part of a political campaign, and legal.

First and foremost it should be noted Vladimir Putin is not a Bolshevik leader. He was not the leader of the Russian Communist Party, Gennady Zyuganov was until he as replaced by Pavel Grudinin in 2018. And it is a successor to the Communist Party of the Soviet Union that was legally banned by the person who appointed Vladimir Putin, Boris Yeltsin. It is now called the Communist Party of the Russian Federation, rather than the Communist Party of the Soviet Union. It is not the same party that was made illegal by Boris Yeltsin, it is still illegal to be a Bolshevik.

Modern Political Economic Conditions by Nicholas Jay Boyes

As a political party, the Communist Party of the Russian Federation seems to be limited to certain political functions, such as taking part in universal suffrage. As is well known, Russian universal suffrage is notoriously corrupt; Reuters has shown this repeatedly, less people voting at a station than reported, multiple voting by individuals. It is generally accepted as Vladimir Putin's party being helped by this, not the Communist Party.

Incidentally the Communist Party used to be involved in more economic activities, like labour unions and cooperatives. The new party seems to be focused mostly on winning the elections, which we have seen are questionable regarding the legitimacy of United Russia, Vladimir Putin's party.

So Russia is no longer a Communist country. As there are people who would suggest there is a harmonious society of the Communist Party and capitalists in Russia, the Communist Party there could be more vocal regarding Vladimir Putin and the capitalists. But remember the Communist Party was made illegal by the very person who appointed Vladimir Putin to power, Boris Yeltsin.

Putin has done more to stop the Communist Party than any president since Boris Yeltsin, who he was picked by to lead capitalists there. The vote Boris Yeltsin won that led to the end of socialism, that he used it too provide legitimacy for his power grab, was a trick. They had no intention of having fair elections. Alexei Navalny, an opposition leader, was not allowed to take part in the universal suffrage in 2018. The bourgeoisie was too worried that it would split the vote, resulting in a Communist Party victory.

Thus when we see the Russian military doing things like interfering in American universal suffrage, we have to conclude it is the bourgeoisie there doing the interference.

How many times did we hear boldfaced lies in respect to the collusion between the American capitalists and their Russian counterparts? Paul Manafort, Michael Flynn, up there in public denying helping United Russia? It looks like all of Trump's entourage universally denied having contacts with Russian military, only to be proven to be not quite so honest. Is it legal to flat out lie to Congress? And if it is not, do they go to jail for perjury if caught?

It also calls into question what Russian support for the Ukrainian separatists was, as Manafort supported the overthrown government that got along with Putin. It makes the war there look like senseless violence for control of markets, rather than a prolonged strike, or labor unrest.

Is it illegal to use foreign military assistance to attain power? Well… They used to say all communists were in Russia's pocket. They said all Marxists were Leninists and if you were a communist you sold out to Russia. If a more worker oriented party had conspired with the Russians to attain leadership through universal suffrage in America it would have been grounds for dismissal 30 years ago. Being a puppet of the Russians was what all communists were called. Who is the puppet now?

So it is something to see Michael Flynn, who led the chants of "lock her up" at Trump's events because of Hillary Clinton's use of a private email server, the accusation being she was compromised to Russia, now greeted by protesters chanting "lock him up".

Russian Interference in American Suffrage and its Results of Late

As it is now common knowledge that the Russians and other Eastern European countries who no longer are part of the socialist movement influenced American universal suffrage, what exactly happened must be examined.

To begin with, the entity called the "Electoral College" would have to be what the Russians were after. By gaining leverage within the Republican Party, they seem to have been able to place a leader in power without the popular will of the people, without the sanction of Universal Suffrage.

How they did this, whether through television, social media, radio, etc. is really not as important as the result; a Casino owner with no experience in government, who was also a Reality Television entertainer, now occupies the White House.

His statements regarding the white supremacists in Charlotte, and the monuments that have become magnets for anti Semitism, have gotten his bourgeois condemned by the United Nations for anti Semitism. And now he suggests he is a friend of Israel, against Iran.

The last time we had a government who did not have the sanction of Universal Suffrage was under George Bush II. That was 2000.

George II was also a bit comical. With him we knew he was a puppet. He was good at taking orders. Donald Trump on the other hand continues to issue bombastic statements daily on Twitter. It's only a few sentences a day, but it almost looks like he has real power. Did the Russians predict this when they interfered with the "Electoral College" resulting in victory of the reaction?

Russian Influence on American Universal Suffrage

For a few billion dollars, some computers and military, the American bourgeois is now headed by Donald Trump. Every day more comes to light about just how close to Russian oligarchs Donald Trump is. Robert Mueller is investigating the matter, and the appointed president keeps saying is it is some sort of conspiracy.

The only thing that resembles a conspiracy is how Russian capitalists were able, with a little money and labour, to get a leader appointed without sanction of universal suffrage in America.

If they wanted a less legitimate representative of the bourgeois, they were successful. A casino owner, with no experience on government, whose money came from a family fortune, and fleecing fools who gambled at his Trump Taj Mahal, now leads the country.

You couldn't possibly discredit American universal suffrage more.

And every day more comes to light about collusion with the oligarchs, yet it looks increasingly distant justice will ever be done. And if it is, Pence will simply be president, even though he was not given the sanction of universal suffrage either.

If a communist had taken power and this was happening when Russia had socialism, what would capitalists have said? Would they have given up democracy willingly?

Russian socialism ended a long time ago. It was traded for western capitalism, and its legitimacy supposedly rested in universal suffrage. But in Russia now we see only one leader, and he has been in power as president or prime minister for 18 years. The opposition, Mr. Navalny, is barred from taking part in suffrage, and he is also a capitalist like Putin.

This is due to Boris Yeltsin and Vladimir Putin. They have not helped out the Communist Party; Yeltsin did everything he could to put down the rebellion, and appointed Putin to continue his efforts to conquer the Russian worker.

It has been successful, now they even have the American president in their pocket too.

Could Vladimir Putin and Boris Yeltsin have done more to end communism?

Modern Political Economic Conditions by Nicholas Jay Boyes

The president being an aggressive capitalist compared to Bernie Sanders should tell us what the Russians really want, free market capitalism.

How anyone could look at Donald Trump and not see collusion is either easily fooled, or ignorant. The only question is if you accept that the Russian oligarchs are now in power in Washington.

Ethics in Government

Almost every day for months Donald Trump has issued a statement on social media suggesting he knew nothing about Russian capitalists and collusion to support his appointment as president.

First we saw Flynn fall, when he got caught supporting the Russian bourgeoisie. He had accepted money and other favors from Putin's oligarchs. He resigned in a humiliating climbdown, and was forced to cooperate with Mueller's investigation.

In the Nuremberg Trials after the war a standard was set. It stated a commander is responsible for his troops, whether or not he knows about what they did or whether or not he condones it. It is still applied today; if a Navy ship has a problem with the crew doing something wrong, it is the captain who has to answer for the crew. The trials also said just taking orders is not an excuse for guilt.

The same applies to Donald Trump. Clearly his staff had collusion with capitalist Russians, and the list of guilty individuals continues to grow.

At some point Donald Trump must be held accountable, and not treated like a fool who has no control over his people, rather as what he is, the Commander in Chief. If his staff acted to get Russian intelligence on Hillary Clinton, as he has stated, he is responsible.

And the evidence is incontrovertible. There is enough of it now to easily show beyond a reasonable doubt Donald Trump received help from Russian oligarchs to deny Hillary Clinton the sanction of universal suffrage she achieved. He even admitted trying to get bad information about Hillary Clinton from Russia, and said it was not illegal, that all presidents take power this way.

At some point justice is going to have to be done. By now his repeated lies to the press, which incidentally he views as legal, have put him in a position that his staff has to tell Europe to dismiss his writings on social media as not a clear statement on the state of the country.

The Tweets are from the Commander in Chief. How they can be dismissed is strange. They obviously come from him. Yet his staff, mostly retired military generals, now suggest we cannot take Donald Trump's social media posts seriously. Was he responsible for Kelly and McMaster, or were they responsible for him? They were supposed to be subordinate, thus the responsibility lies with

Trump. This is his role as leader, if his staff does something wrong, it is his responsibility.

The Nuremberg Trials seem a long way in the past. But they set the standard for ethics that are in place today. Donald Trump, in his role as Commander in Chief, is responsible for his government. His collusion, even if he did not know about it, is something he must be held accountable for as leader. To do any less is to dismiss ethics established in recent history.

Donald Trump and Russian Oligarchs

Suddenly Donald Trump's social media Tweets became real in his meeting with Vladimir Putin. The Donald Trump we had all come to know came out, and exposed a conflicted man desperate to show he had popular support, even though he had not in his appointment as president.

Russia is no longer governed by the Communist Party. The oligarchs now rule, the exploiting class in charge of the means of production.

It is not clear what they discussed, but it must have been the collusion, as the statements Donald Trump made to deny collusion indicate agreement with the Russian bourgeoisie, and this fits with Donald Trump's plausible denial theories, that he didn't know about the Russian effort to get him appointed.

He found a friend in Putin who denied that he was behind Trump's appointment as president. At this point Trump was in above his head. All his social media messages had said he was not appointed due to Russia. Now he was really with the Russian president, he had pulled it off. But he had to make a decision, whether or not to agree with his maker.

He chose to support Putin, and suggest there was not collusion again, but this time he found agreement with the Russian leader. His statements were that he said Putin was not behind his appointment, there was no collusion.

Which of course flew in the face of the Mueller investigation, leading many in Washington to question Donald Trump's decision to support the Russian line that also said there was no collusion.

There were some who said it was just inexperience that led to this, but when you more closely examine the constant social media Tweets about the "witch hunt", "fake news ", etc. and other denials of his collusion with the Putin oligarchs, it fits the pattern. He always said what he told us in Helsinki; there was no collusion. This time all he did was point to Putin and say "see here he is and he denies collusion". Which only supported what the real Donald Trump always said in his Tweets.

Modern Political Economic Conditions by Nicholas Jay Boyes

The interesting thing is his bourgeoisie still supports him. As he is the leader of the Republican Party, you are either on board or not. The exploiting class do not tolerate dissent, and members like Paul Ryan, Speaker of the House, who is retiring but will probably run for president cannot say they supported Republicans but not Trump. If they are not longer in favor of the leadership they should form their own party or try to join the Democrats. There is no other road. They are fooling themselves if they think Donald Trump does not represent what they have become in the eyes of the proletariat, that Trump does not represent their dream president, who even turned the Supreme Court in favor of the reaction.

With this admission of admiration for his friend Putin, the only question left is how much longer his folowing will tolerate this. He invited Putin to Washington, in the face of mounting criticism, some even from his own party about how close he is to Putin. This meeting was later called off due to massive opposition.

Donald Trump and Paul Manafort

It was very strange to see communication from the president, his social media account he uses called Twitter, viewed as not a real description of his feelings. His own following was starting to question his "Tweets", or his comments on social media.

"I have a long-standing policy not to comment on tweets," said Sen. Ted Cruz (R-Tex.).

Washington Post 8 1 2018

We thought the tweets were not of relevance until the president met Vladimir Putin, when the real Donald Trump came out. The social media then came to reveal the real feelings of Trump as regarded his own people, the Central Intelligence Agency (CIA) and Federal Bureau of Investigations (FBI). He proceeded to deny collusion with Russian bourgeois, and pointed to Putin as evidence he was not influenced by Russian oligarchs. He denied the Russians were involved in his appointment, something the FBI and CIA had been saying for months.

Paul Manafort looked an awful lot like an organized crime union boss, helping out what Russia Today panned as a union movement, Viktor Yanukovych, who was really with the Russian oligarchs. RT continually attempted to convince workers on its television station Yanukovych was union, when he as paying Manafort tens of millions of dollars for "consulting".

The sums of money were large, and real. He was not receiving secretaries wages, the way union leadership really works. He had no intention turning down the money, and it was in his interest to continue receiving it.

He was found guilty of eight felonies.

"Manafort, a fixture in Republican politics for decades, was convicted of five counts of tax fraud, one count of failure to file a report of foreign bank and financial accounts and two counts of bank fraud.

NBC News 8 21 2018

After the fall of Yanukovych, Manafort kept the money he received in offshore bank accounts, and used it to live a lavish lifestyle in America.

"Paul Manafort worked for Ronald Reagan, Bob Dole and many other highly prominent and respected political leaders. He worked for me for a very short time. Why didn't government tell me that he was under investigation. These old charges have nothing to do with Collusion – a Hoax!

Donald Trump social media "Tweet"

Donald Trump seems to be suggesting Paul Manafort was not really important. He ran Donald Trump's quest for appointment president several crucial months, and was in the pocket of Russian oligarchs.

"Their attempt to claim obstruction by tweet is really a bizarre and novel theory," he said. *"It's an attempt to infringe of his First Amendment right and ability to communicate with the American people."*

Rudy Giuliani Washington Post 8 1 2018

But on the social media we have the real Donald Trump, saying Paul Manafort was not colluding with Russia, when he supported the Russian bourgeois in Ukraine. Are we to believe Donald Trump's own words?

For a long time it seemed like Donald Trump's social media usage was not really how the president felt. That he was somehow separate from the public when he was ruling. His social media usage not really how he as governing, calling it "Trolling" etc.

Then came his meeting with Vladimir Putin, and reality dawned. He came out, and all the writings he had done became real.

He must be held accountable for his writings. If he is trying to obstruct justice by supporting Paul Manafort, suggesting he was not in collusion with Russian oligarchs, which is what Trump's writings seem to indicate, he should be held accountable to the public. Firing Mueller is not going to make what happened with Russia go away. Here with Manafort they are obviously caught, and Donald Trump has some explaining to do. Attempts at censorship by calling the press "fake news", a "witch hunt" etc. only obstructs justice further. Donald Trump really is who he says he is in his writings, and his style of ruling reflects this.

Politics in America - Donald Trump and Paul Manafort

Paul Manafort had direct contact with Russian and Ukrainian oligarchs, and was paid by them fantastic sums of money. He worked for Trump to get him appointed president, Trump had to have known who he was dealing with. How hard is it too infiltrate Republicans? The epitome of gullible would seem to be the leadership response that Paul Manafort's real dealings slipped past them. They are not that stupid, and his past has come back to haunt him as he is on trial today for tax evasion. Clearly the events are obstruction of justice again by Trump suggesting Manafort was not guilty knowing full well the fortune of Manafort came from Ukrainian oligarchs, who are also like as Russian oligarchs, capitalists Trump is under investigation for supporting by Mueller. After all, Putin supported Yanukovych, and used Russia Today propaganda to support him. Looking at Donald Trump's writings he is totally caught, and ignorance as plausible denial totally ridiculous. He is a grown man, and it certainly looks like he is attempting to obstruct justice about his collusion with Ukrainian and Russian oligarchs.

At the time of writing Paul Manafort was convicted and sentenced to about 10 years in prison for his corruption and lies. It remains to be seen whether Donald Trump will pardon him.

American Universal Suffrage

In light of the recent events that have questioned the leadership of Donald Trump, that he had gotten Russian help to get appointed president, it is probably true. But given the condition of what the bourgeois call "democracy", the problem is more systematic.

The presence of the Senate, the upper house of representatives, is a point. It is comprised of 100 Senators, 2 per state. When they vote they are all equal; Illinois, New York, and California equal Arizona, Nevada, and New Mexico, 6 Senators. But the former comprise the largest cities in America, the latter often just desert like Arizona and Nevada.

So the Senate comprises some of the least developed parts of the country, yet has an equal vote with the cities.

"United States congressional apportionment is the process by which seats in the United States House of Representatives are distributed among the 50 states according to the most recent constitutionally mandated decennial census. Each state is apportioned a number of seats which approximately corresponds to its share of the aggregate population of the 50 states. However, every state is constitutionally guaranteed at least one seat.

Wikipedia United States Congressional Apportionment

Approximately 710,000 people in the Census are represented by a Congressman, so it naturally follows that the House of Representatives is more fair than the Senate, for the reasons stated above.

Then we have the Supreme Court, which is elected by the Senate. The appointment of Supreme Court Justices for life terms, by the Senate, further keeps the most rural and backward members, who are easily controlled by capitalists, in control of the legal structure of the state. It brought us Dred Scott, which divided the nation so badly Civil War was the result. The justices are nominated by the President, and Senate approves them.

Modern Political Economic Conditions by Nicholas Jay Boyes

In the suffrage of 2016 New York, Illinois, and California all gave the popular vote to Hillary Clinton. It was a pivotal moment; the 3 million more people who voted for the first woman to win the sanction of universal suffrage in America than her opponent may very well have come from the larger cities, but due to the "Electoral College" system the popular will of the people was denied to Hillary Clinton.

When viewing the Russian collusion with Donald Trump it is easy to point the finger. A former adversary, a workers state only recently disavowing its proletarian nature, now a friend of the president.

What is a little harder is coming to terms with the real root causes. The bourgeoisie has been using the "Electoral College" method to get appointed president before, George Bush II, for instance. He, like Donald Trump, also did not win the sanction of Universal Suffrage in 2000, yet governed 8 years. At best we can say his second term, after committing millions of young Americans to two wars overseas, in Iraq and Afghanistan, the latter still raging 17 years later, the former not quite so pleasing as a victory, Bush gained the sanction of universal suffrage.

The name of the group of people who has done this twice is calling itself "Republican". Plato's Republic is a fine book that describes democracy in Athens. It survived the burning of the Great Library in Alexandria by the Christians, and is what the term Republic represents. Today's "Republicans" seem to be dictators, who come to power regardless of the people knowing whether or not they won the popular vote.

America's system of universal suffrage seems to be not quite so fair. The fact the Russians have learned how to exploit it should be reason enough to lose the Supreme Court, and the Senate who vote on the appointments. The "Electoral College" also bears blame for this, the person who did not win the sanction of universal suffrage was appointed president again, the second time in 16 years.

It is important to remember this when Cuba has the bourgeois finger pointed at it calling it dictatorship. It is. But just how democratic is America? Are they really a shining example of universal suffrage for the world to see and follow? At least Cuba claims to be in favor of the majority of people there who are working class. The bourgeois make no claim of being in favor of the working class, the have always fought against independent organizations of the workers, labour unions, the Communist Party, ecological groups etc. American universal suffrage may elect the lower house more fairly, but how different is it from Cuba, where local suffrage, like Congress, is the only official suffrage taking place?

The Russian bourgeois probably did interfere in America's politics, but there are reasons why they were able to do this. What we know of as government caused this to occur. But rooting it out would take far more than simply removing Donald Trump.

July – August 2018

Political Economy

Wealth and Production

Money capital representing commodity capital is how commodities are exchanged. A commodity is any item that is produced that is not destined to be used by its producer, produced under social conditions with the intervention of wage labour. Wage labour is the condition of the working class, the proletariat, where the worker is being paid enough to survive and keep on labouring for a capitalist who gains materially from exploitation of this labour. Surplus value is the portion of the day that is worked without pay for the bourgeoisie, the exploiting class. All capitalists produce use values for consumption to create surplus value, which they do not exchange with the worker.

The bourgeois have to be able to use the accumulated surplus value, capital, the stored up labour power productively, or if it is not used it becomes a hoard, and a hoard is not productive. Under capitalism accumulated money becomes capable of circulating commodities, money capital. It resembles a hoard but is part of the production process of capital; it turns over commodities.

The capitalist's fortune is created through the exploitation of the working class, by creating surplus value from his ownership of the means of production. The increasing value of his capital is accumulated without exchange with the labourer, and the capitalist represents the owner of this wealth gained through exploitation.

The first concern is to make a profit, he must do this or he will become useless, and his competitors will be able to better produce commodities as they have invested their capital more productively. Productivity must be constantly rising, capitalist production has to keep improving the means of production, and it is this they spend the money gained by amassing surplus value as capital for.

Taxes are subordinate to capitalist profit. First there is profit, then tax is divided off to the state, and is used as revenue by capitalists, often for protectionist reasons like bailing out the bourgeoisie when their factory is failing to make a profit.

The state also contains the army. Most of the state's money goes to the war machine and police. Another large part of it goes to diplomats, ambassadors, professors, etc., the latter providing the ideological superstructure to promote capitalism. They are part of the bourgeoisie, conscious promoters of the rights of capitalists. The state is used for maintaining wage labour, with punishments for questioning the process of profit production.

It is possible for the state to give in to the workers. Because it is the repressive mechanism, defeat of the capitalist can result in nationalization without compensation. In which case the property no longer produces surplus value, and essentially becomes the property of the workers.

Of course, it is contentious, and rare. Most of the time if something gets nationalized, it is to make it be able to produce a profit again, and the capitalist is compensated massively like General Motors, which was bought by the state, and then when it was profitable again it was returned to capitalists. Creative accounting allows the bourgeois to suggest the company paid back the state, but now the company no longer has to fail if it does not make a profit. Usually the bourgeois nationalize only in conditions of the company being "too big to fail", in which case the Treasuries money is divvied out to support the company until it is able to make a profit again. The investors no longer have to worry if they speculate on GM capital they will lose their ass. When the company discovers it is able to profit again, by using the state to prop up its capitalist production, it is expropriated. It is often done when industry is getting old and outdated i.e. American fossil fuel industry.

When we approach western society it is the labourer who produces the wealth. This happens in production, where all wealth is created. We are starting to see a shift towards ecology being seen as sovereign wealth, as something that does not fit into the capitalist system of wealth.

But the capitalist system is still in control, and it is the production of surplus value that determines what and how much will be produced. The unpaid section of the workday, the surplus value, is what creates the capital accumulation. The accumulation makes greater exponentially the difficulty of the worker ever owning the product he produces. He produces a commodity, a product he does not consume himself, rather is exchanged for enough to survive and keep labouring. He does not control the amount of surplus value produced, or its subdivisions into rent, taxes, etc. This is the position of the worker in the western society, the society of the world market and capitalism.

It is the labourer in the most advanced capitalist societies who can more easily grasp a world beyond capitalism, where the machinery is used for social development of the collective production of mankind, rather than for the creation of surplus value. It is only the experience of having to live in a society where everything is for exchange value, and the universal prostitution it brings, that can make the proletariat realize what and why he must build a new society, where rather he collectively controls the machinery that he is currently labouring on instead of working up products with no real connection to ownership of the collective product.

Thus it is a major leap in consciousness for the worker to even realize what he produces is his own product.

Under the current system the worker has no control over the machinery, which increasingly displaces workers as it grows ever more advanced and productive. His job no longer requires skill; he pulls a lever, pushes a button, etc. as productivity increases. With the accumulation of capital if anything his position becomes more and more precarious as capital accumulates; he can easily be replaced by a 12 year old, as skill goes away as machinery advances. Due to dangers of work stoppages often in England it really was a 12 year old boy working with a power loom 12 hours a day in the late 19th century, and his parents brought him food when he was working and he ate it during what little breaks they gave him.

The industrial reserve army of workers, who always accompany capitalist industrial development, also grows. These souls lie in wait for capitalists to get large orders, when they get a few months labour, and then are again unemployed. They are unskilled labour power, displaced long ago by capital through the advancement of the machinery, it no longer requires skill by the labourer to produce a commodity.

In writing and studying political economy, it is possible to understand how the capitalist system is functioning. The ideas of Karl Marx are probably the most unified of theories about the functioning of capitalism, and David Ricardo and Adam Smith before him also are important.

Ricardo says if wages rise, profits fall. He sees the two as connected, which they are. But profits can rise without wages falling, an increase of productivity that creates more surplus value (what we assume Ricardo means by profit). Otherwise we get caught up in Adam Smith's problems with classifying everything as wages, rent, and profit. There is no category of raw material, machinery, (constant capital). This causes Adam Smith all sorts of difficulties.

Here we return to Ricardo, who said wages rise profit falls and vice versa. An increase in productivity results in more profit, but the value of wages may not change, if productivity simply increased and production increased with it. Now you have more profit with the same amount of wages. Relative surplus value has increased without an absolute rise in wages or reduction of labour costs. More profit without a lowering of wages is the result, and this is not unusual for capitalist production. In fact it is one of the main goals of this form of production to constantly raise productivity. Ricardo should have considered more than simply wages and profit, and added in the cost of machinery. Then at best he could say machinery displaces workers, but it still does not explain if productivity rises and the number of labourers stays the same, production increases without removing workers, as he said less wages and increased profits, and vice versa. If he looked at each unit of production and calculated how much unpaid labour it contained, profits (surplus value) would rise and wages would fall relative to each individual products labour contained in it, or its value. Relative surplus value increases with an increase in productivity, but wages could rise and the profit could also increase without the profit rate falling, if the commodities were produced and both wages and profit rose together, an increase of relative surplus value and wages at the same time. Here we assume Ricardo is referring to surplus value by profit, rather than lumping in the machinery with the surplus value, which causes all sorts of difficulties such as every stage of production has to return the value of the labour previously added to it every time it is sold. The profit rate would fall the more machinery and raw material costs multiplied, as there is less surplus value per unit compared to the price of the product, its value falls with advances in production. The machinery is more valuable, and must be constantly connected to the surplus value, but there is less labour and consequently surplus value when the machinery cost is larger. The rate of profit would fall per unit as well as wages if the constant capital was calculated with the surplus value, as profit. Ricardo's thesis rising wages equals lower profits and vice versa does not hold water.

Ideas of Liberation and Material Conditions

Societies in the less developed world, with less material wealth than the most industrialized countries, were not the societies where many revolutionary ideas were formulated. Karl Marx and Friedrich Engels were from Germany, and exiled to England. They were not from Eastern Europe, which at the time was still dominated by feudalism in many areas. Karl Marx wrote the four volumes of Capital in the London Public Library in the 1860's, and Engels also wrote from London, an advanced industrial power that was firmly a modern capitalist state, like France and Germany.

The ideas of social ownership of the means of production came from the most wealthy societies. It was there people were able to see another kind of society was possible, that the development of the productive forces was reaching a state where there could be something different than the current state of society, that social ownership of the means of production was possible.

Thus it is in the most developed world we see movements rising up challenging capitalism. We have seen this repeatedly, in Catalonia, where the most wealthy regions supported ending feudalism, and making legal workers parties. In England the workers with universal suffrage decided to end membership in the single market.

Both of these movements are taking place in the most industrially developed parts of Western Europe. The European Union has many members that are not as materially well off as Catalonia and Britain. Thus the denial of the Catalans independence movement. Its leaders, who would have left the European Union if they had gotten independence, were forced by Spain to stay in the European Union.

Britain places the European Union in another difficult spot. There it is English workers trying to leave the single market. It is not the Irish, it is the most well off regions of Britain who wanted to leave the single market. All the capitalists have been able to do as of yet is suggest the reactionary bourgeois are responsible for the rejection of the single market, to threaten the worker who wants out of the market he is acting reactionary when he opposes capitalism.

But where is the "Eurosceptic" movement in Spain as of late? If the Catalans would be leaving the European Union if they declared independence, would this not have been a victory for the former?

It was a farce. Spain showed what the reactionary bourgeois really want, the ghosts of Francisco Franco and Phillipe Petain returning, the monarchy supported and capitalism reigning.

If the poorest societies were the most likely to question bourgeois rule, India would have gone first. The peasants live on two dollars a day there. Clearly socialism did not come from the developed world.

In America Cuba, although poor, was able to look into the sky and see the spacecraft take off from Cape Canaveral. Cuba may have been poor, but they were only 140 kilometers from America's border. This closeness gave Cuba a different perspective than El Salvador, or Jamaica. Thus Cuba was able to have a revolution in 1959 that challenged bourgeois rule, and still exists today. As of late the reactionary bourgeois leadership of Donald Trump is clamping the Embargo down, the Embargo that has been annually voted on by the United Nations again and for about the 20th time, the vote resulted in America and Israel being the only countries to support the Embargo. The bourgeois are clearly threatened by their labourers.

In America the revolution has been held down violently for years. The atrocities are so bad most of us who have been on the opposing side of the violence prefer not to talk about what we have been through. It is similar to the Holocaust when the Jewish and the Communists did not want talk about what happened to them. Suffice it to say the weapons are designed to quell the proletarian movement. And they use all of them when rebellion threatens the bourgeois control of the means of production....

So we see it is the most wealthy of societies where the workers have vision to create a different society, but also face the most repressive state, the state with the most accumulated capital, and the workers facing conditions of the impossibility of ever being able to purchase the means of production from capitalists. Ecological ideas follow suit, they too are revolutionary, and it was the most industrially developed nations that gave birth to the ecological movements. Africa and Asia did not create environmentalism, it came from the most industrially developed parts of North America and Europe, the societies that were responsible for the capitalism that destroyed ecology to create profit that has led to the world market, and commodification of all living things.

In this respect we see that the most revolutionary proletariat is in the most capitalist countries, where accumulation of capital makes control of the productive forces by the person working on them least likely. Multi million-dollar machinery, where the worker finds himself labouring, removes the possibility of ever buying the means of

110

production for the labourer. Capital is stored up labour power, in control of living labour. It is these conditions that give rise to the revolutionary proletariat, not simply social inequality. In fact, it is beyond the lifestyle of the bourgeois man of the world that is the main thing causing rebellion; it is the disconnection between the person labouring on the commodity and his ownership of it that is the problem. He labours on a product that is not his own, he has no real material connection to his product or the machinery that was created by the labour of him and other workers, and supported by creating surplus value from production by the capitalist, the unpaid section of the workday whose proceeds do not simply go to a hoard, rather are used to cement the position of the labourer as subordinate to the capitalist.

July – August 2018

Critique of Imperialism, the Highest Stage of Capitalism by Vladimir Lenin

The concentration of capital experienced by Vladimir Lenin in the early 20th century, described by him as an integral part of what he called "imperialism" in the book Imperialism, The Highest Stage of Capitalism, led Lenin to ascribe money capital as the dominant form of capital.

In Capital Volume 2 by Karl Marx it is proven that financial capital, regardless of its seeming dominance is subordinate to industrial capital. Money in circulation produces nothing, whereas industrial capital is where the real surplus value is created. Industrial capital can experience crisis due to the extension of time circulation can have in these conditions. A longer or shorter turnover time of the capital in circulation is part of the cycle of capital turnover. But for instance an increase in production resulting in more commodities on the market, with no way to sell them, causes the crisis. It is not a shortage of money capital that creates the crisis, it is the change in production that affects the ability of the capital to turnover. There are not enough buyers, but this is not due to a shortage of money capital, it is from production.

Lenin saw the banks of Russia dominated by American, British and French capital. This capital was part of the production process in Russia, which, like many other countries at the time, was dominated by capitalists, and the most powerful of these were the western Europeans and Americans.

At the time production was becoming dominated by monopoly conditions, which led Lenin to describe capitalism in a different light than Marx. With the ascension of massive concentrations of capital by a few large companies Lenin thought capitalism had fundamentally changed.

It hadn't. Financial capital was still subordinate to industrial capital. It was just not as obvious to those outside the creditor countries. What seemed to be happening in the debtor countries was the banks were in control. As the money capital was stored there, it appeared to be the banks making the decisions, and through finance capital the banks were running everything.

He neglected the sources of the financial capital (capital in circulation), which was being produced by production. Industry in Russia was still just starting to be totally dominated by capitalists. Britain, France, Germany and the United States were well into capitalism by the start of the 20th century.

Thus the struggles of the proletariat in the most capitalist countries was not addressed by Lenin directly, rather the less powerful countries such as Russia were his focus, at least in Imperialism, the Highest Stage of Capitalism.

In the latter respect the work is good. Lenin saw what was effects of capitalism on the less developed parts of the world, a view that was his experience as a Russian from the turn of the 20th century.

But one should remember the creditor nations were commodity producing nations, and this commodity production is what causes money capital to form. Money capital does not miraculously expand. It requires commodity production, something has to be produced and sold to form money capital. The banks may have some power, but if production fails the banks fail. Credit may ease the turnover of capital, but it more resembles a merchant who speeds up the turnover of capital. And commodities have to be produced to create money capital, which although is an essential part of capitalist production as it affects the speed of turnover in circulation, the scale of production is what creates the market for commodities.

This confusion of the bank being in charge of production is the main flaw in the well-intentioned Russian Marxist. And it was natural that society would appear this way to the debtor nation. But with the growth of the world market the real capitalism of Karl Marx in Capital comes clear.

Karl Marx was most true when it comes to society dominated by capitalist production. And even concentration of capital was not strong enough to change the basic laws of capitalist production written about by Marx.

Crisis

If the world market goes into a period of overproduction, it will affect circulation of commodities. It could be triggered by tariffs on imports, leaving American goods unsalable, overproduction when unsalable commodities will be lowered in value. In the last recession the commodities were stacked up in the ports, unable to be sold. Production cannot continue without circulation of commodities. It is like picking a crop, if it is delayed you lose the crop. Industrial production is the same way, if the train does not come serious problems result, the capitalist loses money every minute the machinery is not moving.

It looked like crisis was starting to come after the tariffs in late July 2018, when the farmers had to be bailed out 12 billion dollars. The market had yet to crash, and the economy was showing signs of growth. The bourgeois had yet to acknowledge the crisis; they just signed off 12 billion dollars, probably mostly to agribusiness. Larger farmers had to own large farms to make a profit, rather than simply work for pay as small farmers. The farm was now was now so big it was impossible to run it without a crew of men with the profit motive, and it came to be dominated by a few big farmers, who got the bailout.

" *the common use of the phrase (bailout) occurs where government resources are used to support a failing company typically in order to prevent a greater problem or financial contagion to other parts of the economy. For example, the U.S. government assumes transportation to be critical to America's general economic prosperity. As such, it has sometimes been the policy of the U.S. government to protect major American companies responsible for transportation (aircraft manufacturers, train companies automobile companies, etc.) from failure through subsidies and low-interest loans. These companies, among others, are deemed "too big to fail" because their goods and services are considered by the government to be constant universal necessities in maintaining the nation's welfare and often, indirectly, its security.*

Here's what we are looking for:

"In the Financial crisis of 2007-2008, large amounts of government support were used to protect the financial system, and many of these actions were attacked as bail-outs. Over $1 trillion of government support was deployed in this period ... The U.S. TARP program authorized up to $700bn of government support of which $426bn was invested in banks, American International Group, automakers, and other assets.

Modern Political Economic Conditions by Nicholas Jay Boyes

In the United Kingdom, the bank rescue package was even larger, totaling some GBP 500bn. Controversial bail-outs occurred in other countries as well, such as Germany (the SoFFin rescue fund), Switzerland (the rescue of UBS), Ireland (the "blanket guarantee" of Irish domestic banks issued in September 2008)"Bank Guarantee Scheme". NTMA., and several other countries across Europe.

Wikipedia Bail-out

Speculation on the ability of workers to pay their mortgage on their house was the start of the crisis. Strange financial arrangements, speculation on mortgage-backed securities (MBS) and collateralized debt obligations (CDO), essentially money capital involved in housing and construction and its failure was part of the recession. Things began to snowball as the money capital failed to turn over commodity capital in the form of residential housing, and the prices of houses plummeted. The banks were sunk in on speculation that their capital would return profits. As housing prices declined, the banks that had borrowed and invested heavily in the mortgages reported significant losses. The banks could not stand the losses as the bubble burst and the houses that were overvalued began to fall in value. They had loaned money they were no longer easily getting back, foreclosures started to occur with increasing regularity. The banks did not have the wealth to pay for the failed mortgages, the money capital was simply not present, resulting in massive bailouts by the Treasury to failing banks.

The banks were losing money as the housing bubble burst, so could not lend money, resulting in money capital becoming more scarce. At this point the central banks stepped in with bailouts, to keep money lending available to capitalists. Money capital plays an essential role in capitalist production, as it is part of the turnover process of capital. Money capital produces no commodity, it is required to turn over commodities from production. Commodity capital needs money capital, and it is without a tangible commodity money capital functions. It is viewed as a cost of production, and compensated by capitalists with a rate of profit comparable to industrial capital. With less money capital available, it was harder to turn over commodities, like in the housing market. The intervention of the state was to keep the commodities turning over, as they were becoming clogged up in Los Angeles's port, leading the port authority to declare LA's port was not a place to park commodities until they were sold. The state used its money, taxes derived from profit, to keep capital profiting. It is a perfect example of the claim on the public money by the bourgeois, the purpose of the state to maintain the production process of capital.

Speculation on the ability of a worker to be able to pay back his mortgage ran rampant prior to the crisis. When the housing bubble broke, the risky loans were defaulted on. The speculators began to lose their fortunes, the money capital was unable to turn over commodities, and commodity capital sat like a hoard, and hoards cost money not produce profit. It is very important that commodities turn over properly, it is like a crop in the field, if it is not picked at the right time, the crop is a failure. Production slowing or stopping altogether means loss of profit. Every minute a machine owned by capitalists is not running is a loss of profit. Supply chains begin failing, this is what we saw in the crisis.

"Federal Reserve Chair Ben Bernanke also defined the term in 2010: "A too-big-to-fail firm is one whose size, complexity, interconnectedness, and critical functions are such that, should the firm go unexpectedly into liquidation, the rest of the financial system and the economy would face severe adverse consequences." He continued that: "Governments provide support to too-big-to-fail firms in a crisis not out of favoritism or particular concern for the management, owners, or creditors of the firm, but because they recognize that the consequences for the broader economy of allowing a disorderly failure greatly outweigh the costs of avoiding the failure in some way. Common means of avoiding failure include facilitating a merger, providing credit, or injecting government capital, all of which protect at least some creditors who otherwise would have suffered losses. ... If the crisis has a single lesson, it is that the too-big-to-fail problem must be solved."

Wikpedia to big to fail

It is not really what you would call a free market condition. It gives capitalists in large banks government assurance that no matter how risky a loan is, the state will just pay it back if the lender is defaulted on. Its sort of like picking who is going to become wealthy, by using the public moneys to prop up the bourgeois in favor, who are basically guaranteed to remain in control of capital regardless of how risky of loans they make. Its not being good at business that keeps the bourgeois in wealth, it is control of the public money and ability to tap the Treasury for it when failure is imminent.

"The largest U.S. banks continue to grow larger while the concentration of bank assets increases. The largest six U.S. banks had assets of $9,576 billion as of year-

end 2012, per their 2012 annual reports (SEC Form 10K). For scale, this was 59% of the U.S. GDP for 2012 of $16,245 billion. The top 5 U.S. banks had approximately 30% of the U.S. banking assets in 1998; this rose to 45% by 2008 and to 48% by 2010, before falling to 47% in 2011.

The concentration of money capital, to turn over commodities, allows for money lending to companies, leveraging whole enterprises with financial capital. But this capital can be fictitious, or at least transient, as we saw when the crisis occurred in 2008. Investors all went to the banks to remove their investments when the bubble burst, a bourgeois run on the banks they did not have the cash for. This is when the state assets were used to subsidize the financial capital industry.

"Since the full amount of the deposits and debts of "too big to fail" banks are effectively guaranteed by the government, large depositors and investors view investments with these banks as a safer investment than deposits with smaller banks..

"A study conducted by the Center for Economic and Policy Research found that the difference between the cost of funds for banks with more than $100 billion in assets and the cost of funds for smaller banks widened dramatically after the formalization of the "too big to fail" policy in the U.S. in the fourth quarter of 2008. This shift in the large banks' cost of funds was in effect equivalent to an indirect "too big to fail" subsidy of $34 billion per year to the 18 U.S. banks with more than $100 billion in assets.

"The editors of Bloomberg View estimated there was an $83 billion annual subsidy to the 10 largest United States banks... meaning the profits of such banks are largely a taxpayer-backed illusion.

Wikipedia ibid.

The concentration of capital is completely fused to the state, with money capital of the state in complete control of by capitalists. In reality it has always been a subdivision of profits, money paid for the states day to day functioning by capitalists. But it is no longer a secret that he public money no longer belongs to the public. Taxes are from profits, and property of the bourgeois to use to make ever greater amounts of surplus value. The state and the company are now blurred together, the money of the state being used to leverage control of money capital, and commodity capital. The state is not a neutral organization, and it is questionable in this condition it can effectively keep laws that are supposed to police investors from becoming used to accumulate capital, to seek revenge on a competitor with fixed lawsuits, etc..

"On March 6, 2013, United States Attorney General Eric Holder testified to the Senate Judiciary Committee that the size of large financial institutions has made it difficult for the Justice Department to bring criminal charges when they are suspected of crimes, because such charges can threaten the existence of a bank and therefore their interconnectedness may endanger the national or global economy. "Some of these institutions have become too large," Holder told the Committee, "It has an inhibiting impact on our ability to bring resolutions that I think would be more appropriate,"

"The banking industry spent over $100 million lobbying politicians and regulators between January 1 and June 30, 2011. Lobbying in the finance, insurance and real estate industries has risen annually since 1998 and was approximately $500 million in 2012.

Wikipedia ibid.

We have the public money being used to keep non metric fossil fuel industry moving and the money capital which it had lost when the banks started to fail. Is there any parallel to the latest bail-out? Agriculture sort of seems more direct than banks or automobile industry. If the crops are unsalable on the world market due to retaliatory tariffs, they often do not have the industrial capacity to save the commodities from destruction, for instance dairy farmers whose cows have to be able to keep giving, regardless of if the milk is salable. The latter was starting to occur in California, where the dairy industry produced for 35 percent of U.S. cheese exports to Mexico. If the product is unsalable it is a loss for the farmer. Mexico's retaliatory tariffs were making California's milk too costly for Mexicans to consume, crisis.

"Our product is perishable. I can't sit on my milk for a month or two months," Mancebo (a dairy farmer ed.) told Reuters outside his dairy in Tulare, in California's Central Valley. "These cows can't be shut off."

Modern Political Economic Conditions by Nicholas Jay Boyes

"The United States is Mexico's leading foreign supplier of dairy goods, including nearly $400 million in cheese last year. Dairy operators in California, the nation's top milk-producing state, are especially vulnerable to Mexico's 25 percent cheese tariffs.(Due to Trumps tariffs ed.)

"California dairies, like Mancebo's, export 30 percent of all they produce, compared with 17 percent for U.S. dairies on average, and Mexico is their No. 1 buyer.

"California accounted for 35 percent of U.S. cheese exports to Mexico alone last year, estimated at 33,600 metric tons (74 million-plus pounds), said economist Annie AcMoody of the trade group Western United Dairymen.

Washington Post 7 27 2018

Political Conditions and the State

"Investor Warren Buffett on Saturday disclosed that the tax legislation signed by President Trump netted a $29 billion windfall to the shareholders of Berkshire Hathaway, the Omaha-based conglomerate he leads.

Washington Post 2 24 2018

I'm not certain what creative accounting techniques the bourgeois use for their finances, but the state is already in debt, and its remaining assets are being speculated on by capitalists as the state is starved of moneys by the "Tax Cuts". Although theoretically lowering taxes would raise profits, if you just burrow the money it is questionable if the capitalists are raising taxes on themselves. After all, taxes come out of profits, thus Donald Trump's statement after the tax bill "I just made you a whole lot richer". But he burrowed the money to pay for it, so in reality he did little or nothing, as the bourgeois still have to separate part of their profits for taxes, just a little later down the road. If he really did want to lower taxes to increase profits, he would have had to do something like lower the minimum wage, the condition of many a worker. Because then more labour can be had for less money. Increasing the absolute surplus value would offset the effect of having to repay massive debt with profits. So it is unclear just what Trump was trying to do, as lowering taxes but indebting capitalists to pay for what was supposedly a way to increase profit some time later looks like a shell game, it is starving the state and speculating on its debts. But it is still debts, debts which come from profits.

The capitalist state has no productive assets, at least none that have not been or are not in the process of being made into private property. Even Milwaukee's flagship recycling effort includes a private company making a profit. It's at the point even the sewer is run by a company, Veolia.

We can abstract all we want about what "Tax Cuts" means, but one thing is clear: taxes come from profits. The fact it is on the paycheck only tells us how much profit the bourgeois made that was paid to the state. It does not tell us exactly how much profit our so-called "better" made from his ownership of capital, but all the taxes tell us is part of the profit that was gained, the level of exploitation by capitalists is not present.

The money Warren Buffet claims to have saved is really all now plowed into the bond market, where the states assets are speculated on. Every bond issue carries interest that has to be paid back, a discounted bill for later. The "Tax Cuts" cost 1.5 trillion dollars, to be paid back by the next government of capitalists. And it will be paid for by taxes, as state money does not make a profit.

So if Warren Buffett has really found a way to starve the state and save what would be his expenditure, what could possibly be removed from the state that was not essential? All the state industry that can make a profit has long since been made private property. The only way Mr. Buffett can say he saved money is by investing in the Bond market. And then his profit comes from raising taxes, which taxes himself, as taxes are a subdivision of profit.

Brilliant move Mr. Buffett!

The repressive aspect of the state continues to grow; the military is growing again. Of course, Trump does not mind paying for that, and Mr. Buffett is not complaining about paying for it either. Considering the "Tax Cuts" are paid for by taxes anyways, what is there too fuss about? A disgruntled worker who naturally does not want to pay taxes, which is really a part of the unpaid section of the workday, a part of capitalist profit?

It shows the level of advancement of the bourgeoisie that this is even panned by Buffett as an increase in profits. It is only by increasing exploitation of the worker these moneys can be raised, regardless of whether or not the worker feels he is being ripped off having to pay taxes, which is really a question of how much profit the capitalist employing him is producing. Does Mr. Buffett really believe he will not have to pay the same amount for taxes, even if it is a few years away? Where does he think the money to pay off the bonds will be coming from? Is there a such thing as state industry making a profit?

In the end he still has to pay, and it comes from profits. These shell games of accountants tell us nothing more than a trophy sum Mr. Buffett owns as capital, stored up labour power. His savings tell us one thing only; the level of exploitation of the labourer is increasing. And it is reflected as a growing amount of capital that can afford to pay interest on its debts even if they go to unproductive expenses like the state.

The Bond Market and Taxes

Increasing Bond issues by 1.5 trillion dollars does not lower taxes.

When the state has industry that can create surplus value, for simplicities sake, profit, it is sold to capitalists. The state is paid for by capitalist revenue, it does not make a profit. Bonds are not investments in profitable activities of the state. The money made comes not from profitable investment in state industry, it comes from taxes.

Taxes are a division from profit. There must be a profit before taxes are paid, otherwise we would not have capitalism, the companies would be owned by the state. State industry does not make profit. Profit comes from capitalist production, from the unpaid section of the workday, the surplus value which forms capital.

The fact bonds result in taxes, although they are kicked down the road, often for the liberal progressive bourgeois to obediently pay back when they are in power, and suggest they are balancing the budget etc. shows the subordination of this more moderate section of the bourgeois to industrial capitalists, who get paid the surplus value on the bonds when they come due. This is being kind. Many of the liberal progressive bourgeois have capital too, and it is parked in Bonds. They also benefit from the Bonds being paid back, and the taxes that pay the interest.

Increasing the amount of Bonds issued is not lowering anyone's taxes. In fact the discounted note is paid with interest, resulting in more taxes being paid, although it is too benefit the section of the population who own bonds, the bourgeoisie.

Protectionism and Bail Outs

In a sign of how the economy is going under the new appointed president, we see:

"The U.S. Agriculture Department announced Tuesday a $12 billion package of emergency aid for farmers caught in the midst of President Trump's escalating trade war, the latest sign that growing tensions between the United States and other countries will not end soon.

"Trump ordered Agriculture Secretary Sonny Perdue to prepare a range of options several months ago, amid complaints from farmers that their products faced retaliatory tariffs from China and other countries. The new package of government assistance funds was announced Tuesday and will go into effect in September.

Reuters 7 24 2018

For a year and a half now we have been told about the fantastic shape of the market under Donald Trump, that the stock market was raging, the value of the dollar was no longer falling etc.

Here we see signs of crisis brewing.

$12 billion dollars of subsidies is no small number. That's practically Wisconsin's entire state budget for the countryside. This kind of massive subsidy again flies in the face of the free market, free trade, free enterprise bourgeois, what they really mean when they talk about what freedom is.

Donald Trump has given welfare to the large capitalist farmers, who cannot make a profit due to the excess taxes on their products as a result of the protectionist tariffs he put on America's neighbors. Is he concerned about how the state's money is being used now?

But when it comes right down to it, why farmers pay much taxes is open to question. They do use the cities roads, railroads, ports etc. when the crops come in, so some taxes make sense as they are users of state industry. But the real reason for the high taxes is to favor agribusiness, and push the small farmer off the land into wage labour in the city. The rebels are removed first, leaving only the supporters of the bourgeoisie behind, which explains why the countryside are such reliable capitalism supporters in the Senate, where the agricultural capitalists dominate with 2 Senators per state, regardless of the population density.

Modern Political Economic Conditions by Nicholas Jay Boyes

The protectionism towards non-metric industry is starting to bite. Does Donald Trump really believe any metric country, the rest of the world, will equally trade metric commodities equally for commodities that were not metric?

It makes you wonder more and more just what is exactly is transpiring materially. On one hand you have a stock market whose performance has been satisfactory to capitalists, with low unemployment, yet on the other hand you have massive subsidies to agribusiness. It can only be called another bail out, with welfare checks for the workers who are most affected by Washington.

It remains to be seen how many more bailouts there will be until capitalists stop trying to suggest everything is going fine. They are going to have to do something as bailouts affect profits, as taxes are from the surplus value. You have to have a profit before you can pay taxes, regardless of if you try to make the workers shoulder the burden, by putting the amount of taxes paid on the paycheck etc. Wage labour is paid enough to survive and continue labouring, the rest is the unpaid section of the workday, the surplus value. The bourgeois knows what is required for the worker to stay labouring, the taxes come from his profits.

It also is interesting it is the public purse that this capital is being used from. There goes America's main industry, agriculture, getting a $12 billion dollar bail out. "Making America Great Again" with welfare checks for those most affected by protectionist trade practices from Washington. The crisis seems to be here already, the bailouts are starting. The capitalist again reminds us the state money is not the property of wage labour.

They started by complaining China was subsidizing steel and aluminum, calling it unfair trade practices, and expecting concessions when they started taxing their exports. Who is unfairly subsidizing industry now?

The hours spent crying foul on Obama's government burrowing... The inability to pass bills due to deficits under Obama.... And that is exactly what Donald Trump did with his tax cuts.

It's not just a question of paying it back; capitalists rarely get their credit ratings downgraded. It's possible in a severe crisis it can be more difficult to pay, America's credit rating was lowered in the last major crisis, the recession. But capitalists generally can pay by raising taxes.

And this is exactly what happens when you issue discounted notes from the Treasury; you pay 5% on a dollar, or in other words, the state gets a dollar today and pays $1.05 for it in 5 years.

That is the basis of the discounted bill market. And given the state is not a profitable investment, if state industry can make a profit it is made in to private property. Its 1.4 trillion dollars in new taxes.

Keeping it looking like a benefit to workers is the job of Paul Ryan. Recently he spoke about how much it would help a worker to have an extra $1.50 a paycheck for their membership at the grocery. And he was serious.

He took down his comment on social media about this when the absurdity of this became visible.

Taxes are an expenditure of capitalists from their surplus value, the unpaid section of the workday. Even Donald Trump said his tax cuts "just made you a whole lot richer" in reference to the bourgeois profits that would follow starving the state of money. What he didn't say was who was really paying for it. It comes from taxes, very directly when you have a deficit and do not expropriate nationalized industry.

The 1.4 trillion dollar deficit will be paid for with taxes. Capitalists are just shifting around capital, more or less to the state. It does not affect wages. It affects what the capital gained through exploitation of the working class will be used for.   The state is the same mechanism used to repress the labourer, it is this he meets when independent gatherings of the working class, i.e. strikes, occur. It is met with the power of the state, and no state organization is independent, if an individual does question it who works for the state he is asking for trouble. This state expenditure is acceptable to capitalists, as it allows for surplus value to continue being created through exploitation of the labourer. Most of the states expenditures are connected to the military in some shape or form, if nothing else state industry favors employing veterans at the Post Office in the written test etc.

So the tax cuts are keeping the state starved and speculating on its debts. It is also a lipnus test of if a state industry can be made private property, if it can make a profit it does, i.e. General Motors nationalized and resold 3 years after bail-out. If the goal is to return capital, the company is expropriated when it does. If it doesn't make a profit it stays in the hands of capitalists as a state industry.

Calling it tax cuts while ensuring that the debts contracted with interest will be paid back to the tune of 1.5 trillion dollars, which has to come from taxes in a few years time, is a contradiction. It is taxes on the next generation of workers who will ultimately be the ones who have to create the profits through labour to pay for the bonds interest. He should have just admitted he was raising 1.4 Trillion dollars in taxes over 10 years.

The Debts of the State and Taxes

They can call it what they want, but it is a farce. The Donald Trump "tax cuts" result in:

"The non-partisan Joint Committee on Taxation said on Friday the measures would add as much as $1.4tn (£1tn) to the $10tn national debt over 10 years.

BBC 12 15 2017

What this means is, 1.4 Trillion dollars, a massive amount of money capital, will have to be paid back one day.

But never mind. Live for the moment.

Discounting notes from the Treasury is what the results of this will be, in what may be the vain hope larger profit in 10 years will make paying taxes by capitalists less painful.

The state is not a profitable investment. State assets that can be run to make a profit are made into private property. Bonds are not productive investments in nationalized factories. The only reason for capitalists to nationalize was "too big to fail", General Motors is a prime example; the company first of all was failing, and needed tens of billions of dollars. It did not make a metric conversion and was no longer profitable, so it was nationalized by Barack Obama.

This in itself does not sound bad. But the price tag was more than 60 billion dollars, straight from the Treasury.

We should have known better. When it happened it didn't sound so bad. But in retrospect we should have known what was going to happen. The minute General Motors could make a profit again, it was returned to the bourgeois.

If capitalists invested money like this as private property the fool and his money would soon be parted.

Nevertheless they managed to prop up some non-metric domestic production, but as soon as it could be made into private property again, in about 5 years, it was sold off.

Modern Political Economic Conditions by Nicholas Jay Boyes

In my studies I have been trying to figure out how the ecological revolution fits in with capitalism.

I have come to the conclusion it does not conform to capitalism.

Capitalism first and foremost has all transactions in society creating surplus value. Even when capital is circulating the industrial capitalist pays compensation for the turnover of capital. It is part of the driving force of capitalism, exchange value as a part of all labour.

Ecology and Capitalist Production

The ecological movement has many things that do not have anything to do with exchange value; it is an independent workers movement to help out the ecology that capitalism has absolutely no interest in protecting. It is truly novel.

The ecology movement values nationalized property, national parks and forests. This is contrary to Adam Smith, who looked at a forest and said there was $50 worth of trees there.

The reason recycling started had nothing to do with profits or even exchange value; it was a real community effort to help the ecology. There was no real penalty for not recycling, but people did it. It was a very effective way of producing raw material for industry, completely new, created by the ecology movement. The fact it became able to make a profit recycling was a side effect. It was capable of being done and making a profit, so capitalism began making a profit, Veolia at Milwaukee's recycling center, for instance. The fact it works under capitalism just means it was an idea whose time had come.

Composting is starting to occur. It is a can by the street that gets regularly picked up by the city, so it doesn't smell. Again we have labour without exchange value at the most basic level, in the kitchen. And again, we have a product, compost, able to be sold that did not come from capitalism.

It starts to add up the ecological movement is not exactly capitalism. The production is often done by nationalized industry, and this is not offensive to the ecology movement either. It is labour without exchange value, and values nationalized industry and land. It does not require a profit to be made off industry.

It will always be the efforts of the workers to collect, wash, etc. the recyclables, and they will never be paid money to do so. Composting is the same way. Composting will never be paid for, it is labour without exchange value. It is not even an effort to make a profit at this point, which is why it is nationalized industry that is doing the composting.

Health Care in America

There has been activity of late regarding the state of American Health Care, which is in the hands of companies that make a profit by selling hospital and clinical visits by workers.

Many employers pay for health insurance, although there were still some that do not, or simply refuse to. The latter was a reason for finding a new job; the employer health care was not paid for right by the owner of the company.

The idea of free health care is being written off as unrealistic by the bourgeois, a cute fairy tale that the government would own the hospital and it would be free. But this is exactly what Canada, Britain, and France are doing and it is working.

The real money flowing into the medical system does not flow directly between the patient and the doctor. There is a phenomenon called insurance, which the workers health is speculated on, and a profit is made from whether or not the worker gets ill. A healthier young person is less likely to get cancer, so it is a safe bet the bourgeois will not have to pay for him getting ill, and this speculation is the basis of health insurance.

What it comes down to is speculation on when, or how long it a man will live or die. If he dies without having to have a lengthy stay at the hospital, it saves money and the insurance speculators made a profit.

And this is the basis of the bourgeois system of health care. And it is viewed as too costly to have a nationalized hospital by the health care providers.

Donald Trump and the reactionary bourgeois who took power without the sanction of universal suffrage have been trying to make the beginnings of nationalized health care, Obamacare, go away. For about 8 months it was constantly debated in the House and Senate. Donald Trump asked a dozen times to repeal Obamacare. He asked so many times it almost seemed like he had support, although Obamacare continued to be popular. As it became clear towards the end without a dictatorial decision Obamacare would continue functioning. The real reactionary bourgeois came out; cut off the money and let Obamacare "implode".

The problems with this strategy began becoming clear in 2018 when about 10 million people enrolled in Obamacare who did not otherwise have insurance. And this was only in the rural areas of America, not Los Angeles, New York,

Chicago. Where were these enrollees? Florida, Texas and Virginia, all states that seemed to be most supportive of capitalism.

A moral dilemma. Without democracy simply repeal Obamacare, but what to tell the people about this exercise of muscle? Even the Senate in the end did not support repealing Obamacare, it was obviously a popular programme, at least with the workers who enrolled in Obamacare insurance exchanges. Removing it was a very obvious attempt to repress the worker who had benefited from the beginnings of nationalized health care.

Donald Trump was determined to make a profit off healthcare. But healthcare really does not produce a commodity, at least not something tangible like steel. It is a cost of production, and has to be borne ultimately by the employer, whether or not the worker personally receives a bill his wages can cover (albeit precariously). In the end it is less profitable for the employer for his worker to be too sick to come to work then to keep him laboring and able to afford to pay for health care. It costs money, and workers are paid enough to keep working, nothing more. It is the capitalist who has to pay taxes, it comes from his profit. He knows how much money his workers need to survive, and maintains them labouring for him by paying them this. The surplus value comes from the unpaid section of the workday, taken without exchange from the labourer. That is the basis of capitalism, it's how capitalists make a profit. But it should be quite obvious the taxman is not pulling for the workers. Taxes are a cost of production, and the state is not a considered a productive expense by capitalists, thus the efforts to pay less taxes. If the state was profitable, which would be something other than capitalism, there would be no problem with indebting the state, and industry owned by the state would not be a burden to capitalists.

But we all know capitalism strives too make a profit off all transactions in society, and if nothing else strives to keep costs at a minimum. Nationalized health care touches on a fetish of capitalism to keep all industry out of the hands of the state. It is an expense of production, but it maintains all sorts of aspirants to bourgeois culture, salesman, lawyers, bookkeepers etc. the Middle Class, and the owners of insurance companies are also well rewarded for keeping costs down by speculating on the life of the worker.

At some point this cost of production could come to viewed as productive, the doctor could be seen as creating labour power by keeping workers healthy, he could be seen as creating a product, health.

But it is not this way yet. Which only seems more strange when the state is viewed as an expense, which is where the cost of health care would simply go anyways if nationalized.

International Politics

Catalan Universal Suffrage

Of late there was an attempt at suffrage in Catalonia, too settle whether the region of Spain would separate. The Spanish bourgeois called the suffrage illegal, and proceeded to attempt to stop the attempt to gauge the will of the people there.

There were bloody red scenes as the Spanish Police repressed the Catalonian separatists. About a dozen members of the police were injured; and several hundred people attempting to gain the sanction of universal suffrage for Catalan to secede from Spain were beaten.

Spain still has a monarchy, and the King Felipe IV has said the Catalonian suffrage was illegal.

Thus if nothing else we see the monarchy confronting a clear lack of popular support for their rule in Catalonia.

There has been little discussion of what exactly the economy is supposed to look like after secession. In fact, we know little about much of anything as the bourgeois press is scared to have a real debate, as the Catalan workers may be against the European Union, the single market capitalism so sought after, after the anthropocentric socialist experiments in Europe have fallen to the EU bourgeois of late.

The European Union contains many countries that still have monarchies, the Netherlands, Belgium, Spain, etc. These monarchies are in the countries that did not have revolutions, like Francisco Franco's Spain, largely due to the presence of capitalists in Europe who were allowed to continue making profits even after the uprising in Germany, and subsequent liberation of the German socialist workers. The European Union has never had any talk of removing monarchies; they accept this in many of the original members of the single market.

The Catalans, if nothing else, have yet to come out in support of the King. They also have not put forth any indication that feudal leadership will be present if they secede.

Modern Political Economic Conditions by Nicholas Jay Boyes

The monarchy and capitalists like Prime Minister Mariano Rajoy were against Catalans too. The democratic socialists may support a united Spain, but they are bourgeois socialists who supported the single market, and are against Catalan independence.

Mariano Rajoy Prime Minister, and the monarchy of King Felipe VI, has made a decision to reimpose Spanish law in Barcelona. At the same time:

"I am happy that thanks to the decision of the Princess of Asturias Foundation, I am receiving tonight the Concord Award for the European Union.

"We met forty years ago, even if he doesn't know about it. I was still a student when I read his brilliant poem about censorship, in the time of the Communist dictatorship in Poland. Together with my friends, we printed this poem in our illegal printing house in several hundred copies. With time, Zagajewski became for my generation a symbol of the freedom of speech, of the independence of thought, and of our longing for Europe - not in the geographical sense, but in political, intellectual and axiological ones. etc...

Princess of Asturias awards 10 20 2017

This is notable as it shows the true feelings of the monarchy towards the European Union. It shows the true colors of the European Union that they accepted the Asturias award.

The Asturias Awards ceremony was held in the midst of the violent response to the peaceful gathering of the Catalans, in which sovereignty of Catalan was agreed upon in universal suffrage. It is surprising as many Catalans took part; the Spanish police reaction was to stop the suffrage. Intimidation of the Catalans discouraged many Catalans from taking part in the suffrage.

What is interesting is the feelings of the reactionary bourgeois as regards the European Union, the anti European Union "populists" have not spoken as of yet, but the European Union has said Catalonia would not be allowed to be part of the single market if they were successful and left Spain. Where was the reactionary bourgeois this time, to suggest leaving the European Union was part of their plans? They have been remarkably absent. The Asturias awards by the monarchy would be their representatives, and clearly the European Union is supporting the monarchy and the bourgeois there.

"The UK prime minister's (Theresa May) spokesman said in a statement: "The UK does not and will not recognise the unilateral declaration of independence made by the Catalan regional parliament.

"It is based on a vote that was declared illegal by the Spanish courts. We continue to want to see the rule of law upheld, the Spanish constitution respected, and Spanish unity preserved."

"UK Foreign Secretary Boris Johnson earlier offered his support to the Spanish PM.

"After a meeting with Portugal's foreign minister in Lisbon, he said: "We don't think, as far as we understand the matter, that the referendum on independence was well-founded in law.

"Therefore we remain very clear in our view that we should uphold the constitutional integrity and sovereignty of our Spanish friends and that's really our commitment and our pledge."

BBC 10 27 2017

Now we have Theresa May, leader of the Tories, forcing Catalonia to stay in the European Union, as.the latter have suggested Catalonia would not be welcome in the capitalist bloc.

Just how committed to exiting the European Union is she? Here again we have universal suffrage, and a rejection of the single market. Is it really possible to exit the European Union peacefully?

Britain should be the last country to force Catalonia to stay in Spain, and consequently the European Union. After the British workers voted in favor of exiting the single market, we have the Tory leadership supporting what looks more and more like a return of Francisco Franco's actions in Catalonia.

How long ago was it when Catalan leaders were victims of repression by the reactionary bourgeois, their leaders imprisoned and violently held down to stop the Catalans from leaving Franco's Spain, and the remnants of monarchy detested by the workers?

Britain still had a monarchy, and supported the bourgeois royalist leadership, even if the workers had unity against it. Clearly the Western European countries, Spain, Britain, Belgium, etc. all still have a monarchy, subordinate to the bourgeois, but still symbolically present.

It's like going back in time to see Spain. America, for all its warts, had not had monarchy for almost 241 years. Yet there it is in Spain, still kicking. Patriarchal rights to land ownership, complete with feudal titles.

And where is Republican France in this argument against Spanish bourgeois rule? Obviously the latest new party of Emmanuel Macron was supporting the monarchy. He too supported Mariano Rajoy, and the reactionaries. There was no talk from Marine Le Pen now of leaving the European Union for Catalans at the time. The reactionaries were totally caught.

July- August 2018

Catalan Independence Movement Gains Sanction of Universal Suffrage Again

In a move to quell the rebellion of Barcelona, Mariano Rajoy's People's Party moved to have a repeat of universal suffrage there a few months ago.

Perhaps it was no coincidence this happened so close to the Christmas, given the Christian support for his party.

"The party has its roots in the People's Alliance founded on 9 October 1976 by former Francoist minister Manuel Fraga.... while he attempted to convey a reformist image, the large number of former Francoists in the party led the public to perceive it as both reactionary and authoritarian."

Wikipedia People's Party (Spain)

Mariano Rajoy, the Prime Minister, had hoped to suggest he had popular support for the heavy handed techniques of repression of the gatherings of the independence movement, especially the violence used when there was a vote to secede from Spain. For months afterward all we heard was there was not a majority in Catalonia who voted to secede; that only 41 % of the people voted, etc. even though the ballot boxes were repeatedly confiscated, and the riot police answered the call for independence with the baton.

The second time we could then see that a majority of Catalans wanted independence. The elections that Rajoy hoped would quell the rebellion ended up with a majority of people ready to stand up to Madrid and the European Union and remove the monarchy and its reactionary bourgeois supporters like the People's Party from Catalan.

The European Union, prior to Puigdemont receiving the sanction of universal suffrage for the second time said that if Catalonia was to separate from Spain they would be kicked out of the European Union. Spain said they would be staying in the European Union whether they liked it or not, that secession was illegal.

The quest for a republic of their own has seen violence used to repress the leadership. Carles Puigdemont, Catalan's leader, went into self-imposed exile after Spain moved to arrest the leadership of the independence movement. Many Catalan's were arrested or beaten by the riot police in demonstrations, which looked likely to continue as Puigdemont's party had the sanction of universal suffrage again.

Notably absent again from the movement was the "Euro Skeptics" who were more reactionary than the bourgeoisie of the European Union. Looks like in Spain they supported the People's Party, they were happy with being part of the European Union if they had a party connected to Franco. There seemed to be no sense of victory at Catalonia having to separate from the European Union, which is what the European Union had said would happen if Barcelona was the capital of a republic. What would seem to be a clear victory for Marine Le Pen, and the other supporters of Francisco Franco, was not acknowledged. Clearly they had no monopoly on desires of the proletariat to leave the single market.

The European Union recognized Kosovo as a republic. It had about a million people living in what was once Yugoslavia, and was part of Serbia. It was repeatedly supported by the European Union declaring independence from Serbia. Universal Suffrage was given as the reason Kosovo should be declared independent.

Now we have the Catalan independence movement clearly in the majority, winning the sanction of universal suffrage. Will the European Union accept the legitimate desire of the Catalan's to leave Spain, its monarchy and its bourgeois? Will Mariano Rajoy call another election?

Mariano Rajoy would later suffer a no confidence vote in Parliament, due to corruption that would result in the democratic socialists coming to power. Pedro Sánchez Pérez-Castejón, who challenged Rajoy in Parliament, succeeded the People's Party leader. In Spain the person who challenges the ruler must succeed him upon victory. Thus the socialists returned to power.

Puigdemont would remain in exile, although the arrest warrant with Interpol would be lifted in 2018 by Pedro Sánchez. Catalan separating would as yet to have occurred.

"Asked by DW whether he supported other independence movements in Europe, Puigdemont said, "Our principle is not to expressly support any of these nations, but we fundamentally support the expression of the desire for independence. That is: All movements that support the right to self-determination are worthy of support in our view."

DW 7 25 2018

International Politics - Catalan Independence Movement Gains Sanction of Universal Suffrage Again

So Puigdemont says he respects small countries that want to leave the EU. Still no "Euro Skeptics" suggesting they are more extreme than western Europe's capitalists in the movement. Perhaps now that Spain has a socialist government we sill see the reactionaries come out against the single market. Predictable? Remains to be seen.

Donald Trump of late is bold faced lying that he supported Brexit before it happened, when he arrived in Britain a few days after it happened and came out in favor if it. Donald Trump would never have been against the EU, he is opportunist. He went along with the referendum after it was passed, and never took the step of reaching out to the British before the referendum suggesting they vote against the EU.

www.ingramcontent.com/pod-product-compliance
Lightning Source LLC
Chambersburg PA
CBHW030754180526
45163CB00003B/1025